Diving and Snorkeling Guide to

Southern California

by Dale and Kim Sheckler
and the editors of Pisces Books

Pisces Books • New York

Acknowledgments

In the creation of this book the author very much appreciates the assistance of Mary Lou Reed, David Reed, Michael Letteriello and the staffs of the dive stores of Southern California.

Library of Congress Cataloging in Publication Data

Sheckler, Dale.
    Diving and snorkeling guide to Southern California.

    Includes index.
    1. Skin diving—California, Southern—Guide-books.
2. Scuba diving—California, Southern—Guide-books.
3. California, Southern—Description and travel—Guide-books. I. Sheckler, Kim. II. Pisces Books (Firm)
III. Title.
GV840.S78S449   1986   797.2'3'097949   86-30445
ISBN 0-86636-078-6

Photos: All photographs are by the author unless otherwise noted.

Color separations by HongKong Scanner Craft Company Ltd., Hong Kong

Printed in Hong Kong

10 9 8 7 6 5 4 3 2 1

STAFF

Publisher	**Herb Taylor**
Project Director	**Cora Sibal Taylor**
Executive Editor	**Virginia Christensen**
Editor	**Joanne Bolnick**
Art Director	**Richard Liu**
Art/Prod. Coordinator	**Jeanette Forman**
Artist	**Daniel Kouw**

Table of Contents

How To Use This Guide

This guide will acquaint you with the best beach diving sites in Southern California. Offshore reefs and other spots that are accessible by boat are not covered here; they are too numerous, difficult to find, and often require elaborate equipment. Should you wish to dive these offshore locations, we recommend you hire a professional dive charter service that's familiar with the area.

Southern California is noted for its excellent public beaches, but not all of its beaches are suitable for beach diving. Each beach included in this reference was chosen for several reasons: consistently good visibility, averaging 10–15 feet; its variety of underwater scenery, including marine life and bottom terrain; its proximity to shore (all are within 100–150 yards of shore); and easy access to the shore. On the latter point, some exceptions were made. Several of the locations along Palos Verdes, for example, have difficult access. But diving off these spots is also good. At some locations, you can drive your car to the water's edge. Getting to other dive sites requires climbing down steep—but safe—dirt paths and stairways.

Several locations, such as La Jennelle Park in Ventura County and the Old Redondo Piers and El Matádor Beach in Los Angeles County, are only known to local divers. Yet these spots offer superb diving that's well worth the long drive.

The dive sites that aren't featured in depth are mentioned in the chapter introductions. However, at the 29 dive sites in this book, you could enjoy superb diving every other weekend for the next two years.

Keep in mind that all sites are subject to ocean and weather conditions. The dive sites will, more often than not, offer good diving, but all sites are affected by poor conditions from time to time. Heavy rain may make the water dirty and high surf can create hazardous conditions. Always check conditions before leaving home and have an alternate dive site in mind.

Finally, know your limitations. Many of the dive sites included in this book are easy to dive, but they do require some degree of skill. Only you can judge your ability to deal with surf and local conditions.

Large reef structures at Christmas Tree Cove in Southern California rise from the bottom as much as 20 feet. A large amount of marine life can be found circulating among the reefs. ➤

The Rating System for Divers and Dives

A conventional rating system (novice, intermediate, advanced) is not really practical on a site-by-site basis for most locations on Southern California. Some divers are very comfortable with surf and rocks, while others prefer a calm sandy beach. Conditions at the locations featured in this book vary considerably. Most of the spots are suited for the novice or intermediate diver who has some beach diving experience. If you haven't been beach diving in California, you should dive only during the calmest conditions at sites offering easy access. You might also consider diving with a professional divemaster.

We do have some recommendations as to which parts of the site are suitable for divers of various skill levels, though. Inexperienced divers should never place themselves in any situation where loss of buoyancy control could result in rapid depth increases. This translates as advice to keep away from walls (that is, near-vertical or vertical dropoffs). Diving on or near walls is considered safe only for advanced divers, or for intermediate divers under proper supervision. Gradual dropoffs present less hazard, and diving on or below the lip of these dropoffs (slopes less steep than 45 degrees) is considered safe for well-supervised novices. The word *supervised* should be understood to mean that a diver is under the direct supervision of a qualified instructor or divemaster.

These recommendations should be taken in a conservative sense, keeping in mind the old adage about there being old divers and bold divers

Several life forms may be new and strange to the visiting California diver. Consult your divemaster if you have any questions regarding potentially hazardous marine life.

Along Picnic Beach, extending southward, is a huge kelp bed, one of the largest along the Southern California coast.

but few old bold divers. It is assumed that any diver using this guide is in decent physical condition. A *novice* diver is defined as a diver who has recently completed a basic certification sport diving course, or a certified sport diver who has not been diving recently or who has no experience in similar waters. An *intermediate* diver is defined as a certified sport diver who has been diving actively for at least a year following a basic course, and who has been diving recently in similar waters. An *advanced* diver is defined as someone who has completed an advanced certification sport diving course, and who has been diving recently in similar waters.

You will have to decide for yourself, of course, if you are capable of making any particular dive depending on your level of training, recency of experience, physical condition, and on the water conditions at the site. Remember that water conditions can change at any time, even during a dive. Penetration of wrecks, diving in caverns or caves, or diving below a depth of 100 feet is considered to be suitable only for advanced divers with specialized training in these skills. Diving below a depth of 130 feet is considered to be outside the realm of sport diving.

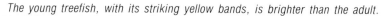

The young treefish, with its striking yellow bands, is brighter than the adult.

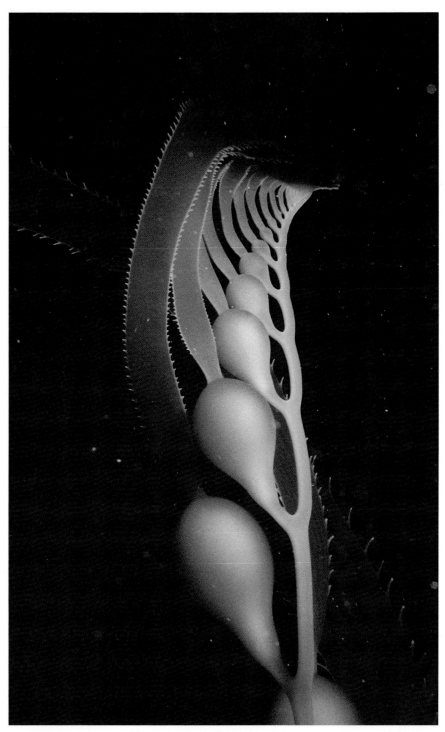

Kelp beds are exciting to explore, but some kelp diving experience is required to avoid entanglement. Always dive with a knife and a buddy.

1

Overview of Southern California

Southern California offers numerous attractions for divers, including a Mediterranean-like climate and a changing shoreline dotted with numerous coves and isolated beaches. This region offers diving opportunities for all levels of divers.

Climate. Southern California is noted for its sunny weather, but many tourists associate sunshine with warm temperatures. Inland temperatures are warm throughout most of the year but along the coast, temperatures can become quite cool. If you'll be staying along the coast, bring along a warm jacket. From December to March, coastal temperatures range from 40–60 degrees Farenheit. You should also carry an umbrella, as this is the rainy season in California. Temperatures rise slightly from April to early July, but expect fog and clouds during the morning and evening. From July to October, the weather is absolutely perfect—warm temperatures, clear skies, and clear waters. Although you can dive Southern California year round, the best time to dive is late summer and early fall. There are few storms and water visibility is generally good.

Water Temperatures. Water temperatures follow the same cycle as air temperatures: 50–60 degrees Farenheit in the winter and 60–70 degrees in the summer. Deeper waters are obviously colder. With these water temperatures, you may want to wear a wetsuit. Some divers get by with a full-length tropical dive suit during the summer, but a full one-quarter inch wetsuit and hood are recommended.

Beach Diving. Beach diving has several advantages over boat diving: it's cheap and you can dive when you want and for as long as you wish. There are just a few guidelines to follow in preparing for a beach dive, and some diving techniques to keep in mind. Beach diving doesn't require a lot of physical strength, but you should have enough stamina to get in and out of the water, reach your offshore destination, and be able to handle an emergency. The best way to get in shape for beach diving is through some kind of aerobic exercise—running, cycling, dance, and swimming.

Southern California is well known for its sunny, pleasant climate as well as its versatile diving opportunities. Divers of all skill levels who enjoy wandering through majestic kelp forests, exploring the intricate reef systems, or just photographing the many colorful marine subjects will find great satisfaction diving along the Southern California coast. ➤

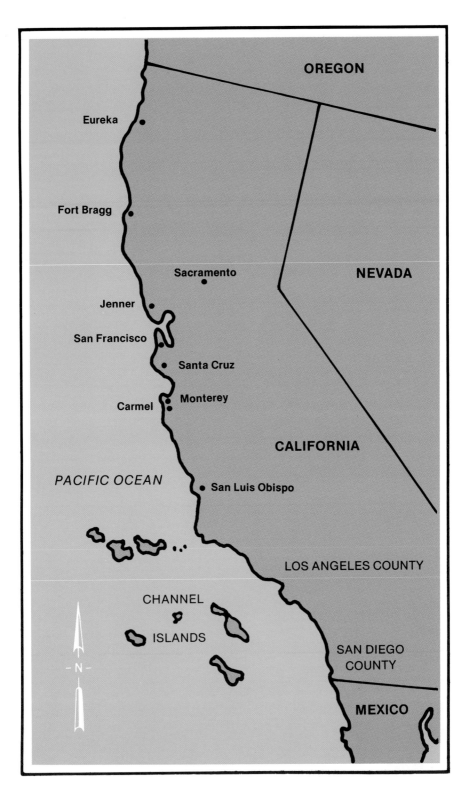

Try to schedule your dives for the morning. The sea tends to be calmer this time of day, and there are smaller crowds. Also try to plan your dives during periods of high or incoming tides. The incoming tides bring in the clear offshore waters, creating better visibility. The higher water may also help you get by a shallow reef on your swim out to the dive site. However, there are some limitations when diving during high tide. Some beaches may become impassable and the surf may be more difficult to handle.

Upon arrival at the beach, take time to carefully observe conditions. Use binoculars to scout out hidden reefs or kelp beds. Watch the surf carefully. Surf will often come in "sets" of two to five big waves, followed by about 10 minutes of small waves. Time these sets. Look for rip tides, which can get you offshore quickly. Carefully check entry and exit points and always have alternative entry/exit points in mind. Observe how the kelp is lying; this is a good indication of currents.

Waste no time entering the surf zone. Do not stop to adjust gear or look back. Swim out past the surf then rest. This will reduce your chances of getting knocked down. Should you fall, stay down. If the water is deep enough (2–3 feet), kick out the rest of the way. Many experienced divers wade out to this depth and turn to swim. Take the larger waves by going underneath them. If you time your entry properly and don't stop in the surf zone, you probably won't have any problems.

To exit the water, simply reverse the process. Approach the seaward side of the surf zone as closely as possible and wait there. Relax and catch your breath. Again, time the waves. Head for shore between wave sets.

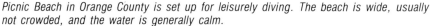

Picnic Beach in Orange County is set up for leisurely diving. The beach is wide, usually not crowded, and the water is generally calm.

Horn sharks are popular in the more rocky areas of California.

Waste no time and don't stop. When you reach waist-deep water, stand up and back out, keeping your eye on the surf. If you get knocked down and can't get up, stay down and crawl in.

Kelp. Giant kelp beds, some extending up 100 feet from the bottom, are typical in Southern California. Kelp grows very quickly, creating dense submarine forests which harbor a variety of fish and invertebrates. Kelp is only hazardous if you don't know how to deal with it. Perhaps the most important thing to remember is that kelp breaks easily. To avoid becoming tangled, keep your dive gear—fin straps, knives, and other tools—close to your body. Keep enough air in your tank to surface clear of the kelp. And always stay close to your dive buddy, so he can help free you. If you must pass through kelp on the surface, do so by crawling and clearing a path in front of you. Most important, *don't panic.*

Hunting. California offers some of the best underwater hunting in the world. Succulent lobster, tender abalone, and game fish of all types can be gathered here. In all locations, strict game laws protect marine life. It's your responsibility to become familiar with the regulations and obtain the proper licenses. At local dive stores you can get information regarding fishing licenses and specific hunting regulations.

Dive Stores. There are many dive stores in Southern California, and some of them sponsor trips to local beaches, often free to divers. A complete listing of Southern California dive stores is included in the Appendix.

2

Diving in Santa Barbara County

Diving the Santa Barbara County coastline can be quite different from coastal diving farther south in California. Perhaps the largest noticeable difference is in the types and varieties of sea life. Colors and sizes are more varied and every crevice and rock seems to hold a surprise. The southern coastal diver should not miss the diving this area has to offer.

From the San Luis Obisbo/Santa Barbara County line southward around Point Arguello and Point Conception, there is little or no coastal access with the exception of Jalama Beach County Park north of Point Conception. Point Conception has been called the "Cape Horn of the Pacific" because of the heavy weather that frequents the area including Jalama Beach. Around the "Horn" of Point Conception is Gaviota Beach. Here the beach access is good but diving is over mostly sand. Down the coast from Gaviota, the next good beach access is at Tajiguas. This small sandy cove offers easy entry, good diving and escape from crowds. Only a mile or so farther south is Refugio State Beach with excellent facilities and good diving.

Continuing south water visibility worsens. El Capitan State Beach, like Refugio, has excellent facilities but only average diving. The next nearest shore access is in the Isla Vista/Goleta Bay area but water visibility is only fair and the water is sometimes covered with oil from a natural seepage from nearby Coal Oil Point.

Arroyo Burro State Beach has cleaner water and good access. Facilities here are also very good. At Mesa Lane, however, facilities are lacking but the diving is some of the best in the county. Farther toward the harbor, there are two or three access points but water becomes progressively less clean. Lead-better Beach adjacent to the harbor breakwater has some interesting reefs and good facilities but normally visibility is poor.

There are few dive spots south of Santa Barbara Harbor. Patches of kelp mark small reefs along the coast. Some of these reefs can be found at Shefield Drive in Mentecito where access is limited. There is a large reef at Carpenteria Beach but the best diving is a long swim away.

Santa Barbara offers a greater variety of sea life than other areas of Southern California. Good diving can be found at Tajiguas (1), Refugio Beach (2), Arroyo Burro (3), and Mesa Lane (4). ➤

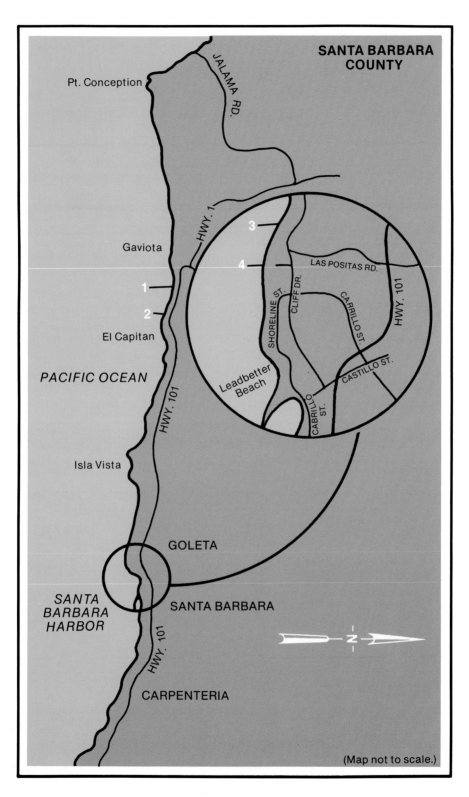

SANTA BARBARA
COUNTY

Pt. Conception

JALAMA RD.

HWY. 1

Gaviota

3

4

LAS POSITAS RD.

1

2

SHORELINE ST.

CLIFF DR.

CARRILLO ST.

HWY. 101

El Capitan

PACIFIC OCEAN

Leadbetter
Beach

CABRILLO ST.

CASTILLO ST.

CASTILLO ST.

Isla Vista

HWY. 101

GOLETA

SANTA
BARBARA
HARBOR

SANTA BARBARA

N

HWY. 101

CARPENTERIA

(Map not to scale.)

Typical depth range	:	45 feet
Access	:	Dirt path
Water entry	:	Sandy beach
Snorkeling	:	Good

It's easy to understand why diving and other leisure activities abound at the state beaches along the coast north of Santa Barbara. The state beaches offer excellent facilities, including restrooms, camping, showers, and food service. But expect large crowds. To escape the crowds and enjoy fine diving, try Tajiguas.

A series of rocky ledges lie directly off the beach and extend to the west. The ledges begin in shallow water and run parallel to shore to depths of 40 feet. Most of the rocks are low-lying, rising 3–5 feet from the bottom. Despite their low profile, some of the ledges extend out five feet, creating large overhangs. This is an excellent area for macrophotography. You may find clumps of yellow, pink, and lavender corynactis anemones, as well as white-spotted rose anemones, with vivid red bodies and tentacles, and large rose anemones, characterized by white tentacles and a deep red body. A small community of red, brown, and California golden gorgonians can be discovered on the deeper reefs. Also expect to find the brilliant orange and blue Spanish shawl and white and gold horned nudibranchs.

The large rose anemone, not common to the southern sections of the coast, can be found at Tajiguas.

Bright colors are common along the Santa Barbara coastline. Many colorful species enjoy posing for photographers.

Fish are a little sparse in the area, but look under the rock ledges for rockfish and around the kelp beds for game fish. Abalone and lobster are also present, though the area has been worked over heavily. Scallops can be found on reefs in deep-water areas that are somewhat inaccessible.

Entry to the beach is on the south side of Highway 101. Parking and access are not visible from the north-bound lanes. If you're traveling northbound on Highway 101, turn around at the gas station located approximately two miles north of Refugio State Beach. Park next to the highway on the dirt areas. A dirt path across the railroad tracks leads to the beach. The path is safe and easy to travel, even with heavy gear. There are no facilities on the beach or near the parking areas.

The best diving and entry can be found at the west end of the beach. Surfers congregate at the eastern end. Although the beach is sandy, there are cobblestones in the surf, particularly in the winter. There is also access farther west on the road that leads to the west side of the point. The incline is steep and sometimes treacherous, but it shortens the swim to the outer kelp areas.

Water conditions at Tajiguas are usually good. Thanks to a mild current, visibility is often better than at beaches farther south, averaging 10 feet.

Typical depth range	:	10–40 feet
Access	:	Sandy beach
Water entry	:	Surf entry from sandy beach
Snorkeling	:	Good

Refugio Beach beckons the leisure diver. The secluded beach, dotted with majestic palm trees, is a perfect spot for an afternoon picnic. There are also excellent camping facilities—including 109 campsites, restrooms, showers, and eateries—plus good diving. In fact, you could have a terrific time without even getting wet. But if good diving is what you had in mind, you've come to the right place.

Refugio State Beach is located approximately 25 miles north of Santa Barbara off Highway 101. Turn off the highway at the ramp marked Refugio Beach and follow the signs. Once through the gate, you'll pass under railroad tracks. Turn right for the northwest end of the beach; turn right for the southeast beach. There's ample parking close to the water's edge, but there is a fee for entering the park.

Kelpfish, as well as rockfish and lobster, are popular at La Jolla Cove. Look closely in the reefs, but do not remove any marine life. It is prohibited.

Orange anemones are popular at Refugio Beach in Santa Barbara County.

Reefs and kelp lie 50 yards from shore. The variety of terrain and sea life is sure to delight divers at all levels. At the southeast end of the beach near the camping area, kelp beds line a rocky bottom. Just 20 feet deep, this is an excellent area for snorkeling, particularly in calm weather. Beyond the kelp are a series of jagged rock ledges that run parallel to shore. The ledges rise 12 feet from the bottom in some spots, creating overhangs that attract unusual species of marine life. Look on the ledges for nudibranchs and on the sandy bottom for sea porcupines and the sea mouse. Anemones lend a splash of color to the reefs, and sea hares (sea slugs) are everywhere.

The kelp beds attract few game fish, and those that can be found—such as the kelp bass—scare easily and are difficult to approach. You won't find any abalone near the reefs at the eastern side of the beach. If hunting is your thing, you'll have better luck along the coast toward the northwest and around the small point.

In this area, kelp is attached to low-lying reefs in 15–25 feet of water. In some places you'll discover an occasional abalone or lobster. This area is best suited to divers who are in good physical condition because it's a long swim from the beach. Nearby reefs can be reached by inflatable boat, which you can launch from the beach in calm weather. Parking is situated a few yards from the beach. And, although the beach is somewhat protected from rough conditions coming out of the northwest, it's a good idea to check conditions ahead of time.

The only drawback to diving Refugio State Beach is the summer crowds. If you plan to camp during your stay, be sure to make reservations early in the season.

Typical depth range	:	10–45 feet
Access	:	Sandy beach
Water entry	:	Surf entry from sandy beach; some rocks in surf
Snorkeling	:	Fair

Near the Santa Barbara city limits, Arroyo Burro State Beach offers perhaps the best diving and the easiest access in Southern California. Arroyo Burro is neatly tucked into a small canyon about four miles north of Santa Barbara Harbor. Facilities include picnic tables, restrooms, and a small restaurant and snack bar. Local dive instructors use this site for check-out dives.

The best diving is to the south of South Point. Getting to the Point requires some walking, but the sandy beach makes it a pleasant stroll. The bottom is mostly sand directly off the beach. But approximately 25–50 yards offshore of the Point, a series of rock ledges begin in 10–15 feet of water. Look under these ledges for colorful anemones, nudibranchs, and other invertebrates. Garibaldi, lingcod, sheepshead, calico bass, and halibut are also present.

Divers headed for Mohawk Reef often enter here. A large reef structure, Mohawk begins at South Point and extends south past Mesa Lane beach. However, the best dive spots on this reef are a long swim out. And because of the location of the reef, the best visibility is to the south, averaging 15 feet.

This small crab has a crop of fungus on its back, for camouflage or food. Other marine life at Arroyo Burro includes nudibranchs, Garibaldi, and halibut.

Mesa Lane 4

Typical depth range	:	15–35 feet
Access	:	Stairway
Water entry	:	Surf entry from sandy, somewhat rocky, beach
Snorkeling	:	Good

As you'll soon realize, finding clear waters along the Santa Barbara coast isn't always easy. At Mesa Lane, though, a reef makes this dive site one of the best in the county for sightseeing and photography.

Until recently, diving here was limited to boats or sure-footed divers who could negotiate the steep, treacherous path that led to the beach. This path has since been replaced by a staircase, albeit long and steep. But at least you can leave your hiking boots home!

You get an excellent view of the diving area from the top of the stairway. There are a number of entry and exit points on the rock-strewn sandy beach. Offshore, kelp beds mark the best reefs, including Mohawk Reef, which extends in sections from north to south.

A small reef line begins within 25–50 yards of shore and extends in both directions along the coast. Much of the kelp you see 50–100 beyond the reef is new. Much of the kelp on the reef was destroyed years ago.

Small caves, huge rocks, large ledges, and overhangs are among common features. The reef rises about 15 feet above the bottom, which varies from 25–30 feet in depth. Depths drop to 40 feet just outside the kelp.

A large rose anemone, with its reddish body and white tentacles, stands among the rocks. Many ledges and caves make up Mesa Lane.

3

Diving in Ventura County

Most local divers prefer the beautiful islands off the coast of Ventura County to the area's shore-diving spots. If you have only a few hours to dive, or don't want to spend money on a boat trip to one of the islands, the dive sites in Ventura County offer easy access, superb diving conditions, plenty of game fish, and spectacular underwater scenery.

Rincon Beach Park starts at the Ventura/Santa Barbara County line. Water visibility is generally poor from here to the Ventura city line. Nearby Punta Gorda offers easy access from a pier that extends to an artificial oil island. There's also diving at other oil piers to the south and in and around kelp beds located offshore.

There's little diving to be had at Pierpoint Bay due to heavy surf, although halibut and pismo clams can be found here and to the south of the harbor. At Port Hueneme lies the sunken luxury ship, *La Jennelle*. The wreck is filled in with rock and lies at the edge of the Hueneme submarine canyon. *La Jennelle* offers some of the best—and least known—diving in Southern California.

South of Port Hueneme, access is limited and diving is mainly over sand until you reach Point Mugu. There are a few offshore reefs, but many are located far from shore. The one exception is a reef at Deer Creek Road. Kelp beds are 30 yards off shore and access is easy.

Just before you reach the Los Angeles County line, there is another reef close to shore of Yerba Buena Road. However, the heavy surf here attracts many surfers. A short distance down the road is Harrison's (County Line) Reef. Lying 300 yards offshore from the blue-roofed apartment buildings, it is recommended for good swimmers only.

With Ventura County's fairly easy beach access, diving in most spots offers game, beautiful underwater scenery, and good diving conditions. The sunken ship La Jennelle (5), is not often visited, yet it is an exceptional site. At Deer Creek Road (6), good diving is only a short swim away. ➤

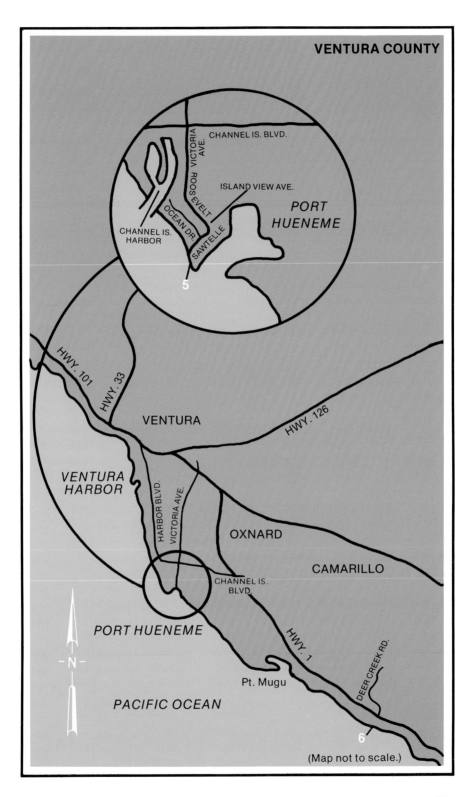

VENTURA COUNTY

CHANNEL IS. BLVD.

VICTORIA AVE.

ROOSEVELT

ISLAND VIEW AVE.

OCEAN DR.

SAWTELLE

CHANNEL IS. HARBOR

PORT HUENEME

5

HWY. 101

HWY. 33

VENTURA

HWY. 126

VENTURA HARBOR

HARBOR BLVD.

VICTORIA AVE.

OXNARD

CAMARILLO

CHANNEL IS. BLVD.

PORT HUENEME

N

HWY. 1

DEER CREEK RD.

Pt. Mugu

PACIFIC OCEAN

6

(Map not to scale.)

Typical depth range	: 10–50 feet, deeper in submarine canyon
Access	: Easy access from rocky beach
Water entry	: Rocky beach
Snorkeling	: Good

La Jennelle Park at Port Hueneme is Ventura County's best dive spot, if not one of the best along the Southern California coast. Ironically, few outsiders know of this site. It shouldn't be long before divers of all skill levels discover this marvelous area, where Hueneme submarine canyon comes to the edge of park, creating good diving conditions and some interesting wreck diving.

The park is named for the 467-foot luxury liner that ran aground on April 13, 1970. Instead of being salvaged, the vessel was surrounded with rock and concrete. As a result, very little of the ship remains exposed. But the peninsula it created at the mouth of Port Hueneme shelters a protected swimming area, which is now home to a variety of fish.

To reach the park, exit Highway 1 in Oxnard to Channel Islands Boulevard. Proceed west through Oxnard to the town of Port Hueneme. Turn left on Victoria. The road runs adjacent to Channel Islands Harbor and changes to Roosevelt as it swings to the left. Follow Roosevelt until it becomes Island View Avenue. This dead-ends into Sawtelle Avenue, where you turn right. At the end of Sawtelle Avenue is a gate on a small road that leads to the beach. Proceed through the gate to the small parking lot. La Jennelle Park and the diving area are to the south.

One of the best features of this dive site is the easy water entry. Follow the block wall and fence that face the beach. This will bring you to a large hole in a tattered chain link fence. Enter from a point just a few feet down the rocks, adjacent to the breakwater. The water here is usually tranquil, except when southerly swells reach inside the harbor. You can also enter the water from the rocks at various locations.

In front of the short pier is a small reef covered with kelp. This is a good area for snorkeling and check-out dives when the water is clear. Along the jetty, the bottom drops gradually to 40 feet. Beyond the edge of the jetty, the bottom drops quickly into the submarine canyon.

Kelp beds cover the rocks in the shallow waters, providing a refuge for Garibaldi and other varieties of fish. The best selection of fish can be found in deeper water near the end of the breakwater. Red and orange gorgonians add a splash of color, as do starfish, anemones, sea urchins, and other invertebrates. Sheep crabs are also common.

Occasionally you'll see a lobster near the rocks and the submarine canyon has been known to attract some large fish. If you venture into the canyon, do be careful. The bottom drops off quickly and you'll need to stay clear of the harbor mouth. Loose boulders can be found on the canyon slope at 70–80 feet.

Around the tip of the jetty the water becomes shallow near the rocks, and heavy surge makes diving difficult. But the shallow area inside the park, across from the beach, offers excellent snorkeling conditions.

In and around the gorgonian at La Jennelle are a number of small fish that make this area their home. Pictured here is the shy island kelpfish.

Typical depth range	: 15–35 feet
Access	: Short stairway to beach
Water entry	: Surf entry from sandy beach
Snorkeling	: Fair

At the farthest point south along the coastline of Ventura County, near Point Mugu, the shore becomes rugged and rocky. At some points, Highway 1 comes very close to the water's edge, but access is still limited. Enter the beach from a short stairway where Pacific Coast Highway intersects with Deer Creek Road. From the top of the stairs you can see a series of kelp beds 50–300 yards offshore. The stairway leads to a sandy beach where surf entry is possible. Reefs that are free of kelp are situated about 50 feet out in 15 feet of water.

A thick kelp bed stretches out 200 yards from shore to a depth of 35 feet. The rich kelp hunting ground harbors bass, sheepshead, and opaleye. Nudibranchs, sponge, urchins, starfish, lobster, abalone, and rock scallops can be found on the rocks. Check the sand adjacent to the reefs for large halibut and rays. The lucky diver may also encounter dolphins, seals, or a gray whale on the seaward side of the reef.

Deer Creek Road is a rocky dive area with large kelp patches within 200 yards of shore. The access to the beach, however, can be limited.

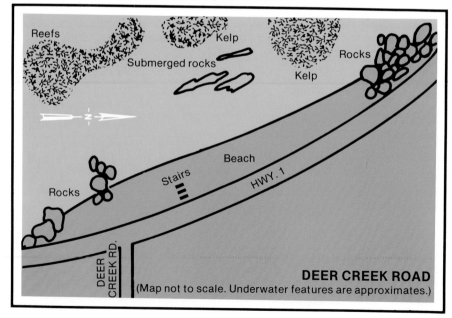

26

The macro photographer can seek out the contrasts in colors common to diving in Ventura County. At Deer Creek Road, larger sea life, like seal or dolphin, may also be seen.

Although the reefs come in fairly close to shore, the better diving is only a short swim away. The spot is open to heavy surf, so be prepared for changes in surge and visibility. With a two- to three-foot swell, visibility beneath the kelp averages 10 feet; outside the reef, visibility reaches 20–30 feet. A high surf that creates a bottom surge can reduce visibility significantly.

4

Diving in Los Angeles County

Once past the Ventura/Los Angeles County line, offshore reefs covered with kelp become more common. A quarter mile from the county line and 200 - 300 yards offshore is Harrison's Reef, a good dive spot if you don't mind the long swim out. This spot marks the beginning of the reefs that lie parallel to Leo Carillo State Beach. Here the kelp comes to within 25 yards of the sandy shore, but water is sometimes murky. The best dive site in the park is off Sequit Point and the adjacent cove to the south. Off Sequit Point, the bottom is varied with reefs supporting healthy kelp and abundant sealife. Because the bottom is largely rock, visibility is usually good. Farther south, the kelp begins again at Nicolas Canyon. Access is good, but it's a long swim out to the kelp.

A lesser-known spot is El Matador Beach. Access is not easy as at Leo Carillo, but it's safe. Kelp comes to within a few yards of the beach, and underneath the kelp farther out is an interesting reef in moderately clear water. Trancas Beach is the next access point to the south, and is excellent for halibut hunting but little else. Zuma Beach, as well as Westward Beach, are fun dives with large sand dollar beds, pismo clams, and sometimes large surf. At Point Dume, a submarine canyon brings clear water and varied marine life in close. But the dive is only for the experienced, as treacherous currents plague the area. Around the point, there is access to Dume Cove but visibility averages less than 10 feet. Little Dume offers similar conditions. Visibility at both of these locations improve somewhat outside the kelp. Paradise Cove and Escondido Beach have poor visibility. Coral Beach is frequently used by instructors for check out dives but, again, visibility is only mediocre. In the Malibu Road area, just north of Malibu Point, visibility improves a little.

Divers visiting the Los Angeles area will find excellent kelp diving off Sequit Point near Leo Carillo State Beach (7). Areas farther south offer good diving as well, but access may be more difficult. Other dive sites along the Los Angeles coast include: El Matador Beach (8), Old Redondo Pier #2 and Redondo Submarine Canyon (9), Old Redondo Pier #3 (10), Malaga Cove (11), Haggerty's (12), Flat Rock (13), Christmas Tree Cove (14), Point Vicente Fishing Access (15), and White Point (16). ➤

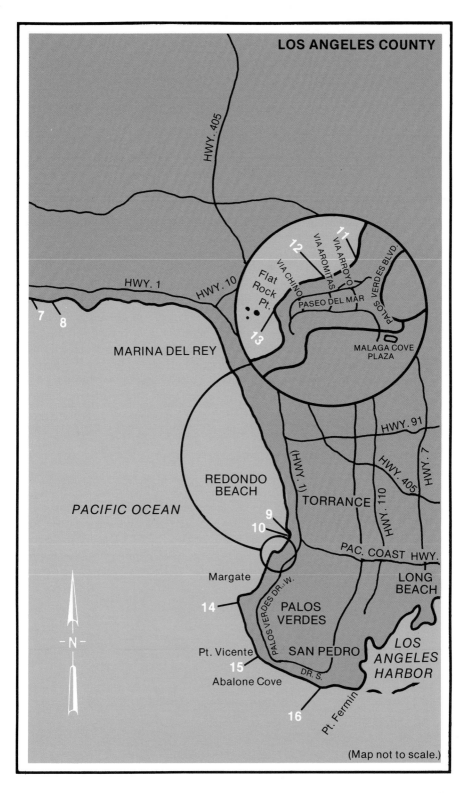

LOS ANGELES COUNTY

HWY. 405

HWY. 1

HWY. 10

7 8

MARINA DEL REY

11
12
VIA ARROYO
VIA AROMITAS
VIA CHINO
Flat
Rock
Pt.
13

PASEO DEL MAR

PALOS VERDES BLVD.

MALAGA COVE
PLAZA

HWY. 91

(HWY. 1)

HWY. 405

HWY. 110

HWY. 7

REDONDO
BEACH

TORRANCE

PACIFIC OCEAN

9
10

PAC. COAST HWY.

Margate

LONG
BEACH

-N-

14

PALOS VERDES DR. W.

PALOS
VERDES

SAN PEDRO

LOS
ANGELES
HARBOR

Pt. Vicente

15

Abalone Cove

DR. S.

16

Pt. Fermin

(Map not to scale.)

29

The Santa Monica Bay, or South Bay as locals call it, is a long, almost unbroken stretch of beautiful sand beaches. Interesting diving can sometimes be had near the piers, but don't go in if prohibited. Artificial reefs present another alternative. All but one must be reached by boat. There is a lesser-known artificial reef at 24th Street in Hermosa Beach that is within 200 yards of shore; however, there's little left of it. A dive off the outside of the large Redondo Breakwater may reward you with some lobster, but heavy surge and a walk over large boulders can be a problem. Diving near the present-day pier or near the harbor mouth is prohibited.

Years ago, there were three piers off Redondo Beach. The remains of these piers can be found today on the sea floor. Old Redondo Pier #2 came to the edge of the Redondo submarine canyon located off Veteran's Park. At Topaz Street, about one-quarter mile south, is the Old Redondo Pier #3. At both these locations, visibility is usually good and the pier pilings are encrusted with anemones. The sand beaches continue southward to Torrance Beach. The coast becomes more rocky at the south end of this beach, where the shore turns west to form Malaga Cove. Here, excellent diving of the Palos Verdes area begins.

Palos Verdes is, unfortunately, also surrounded by cliffs, making access to the water sometimes difficult. There is good access to Malaga Cove via a steep paved path and good diving over parallel reefs. The access to Haggerty's is more difficult, but the diving is better. Turning the corner at Flat Rock Point brings you to even better diving but increasingly difficult access. Across Bluff or Paddleboard Cove is the cliff area known as Margate. Although there are some trails here, a boat is recommended. A few more coves southward is Christmas Tree Cove. From here to Point Vicente, shore access points are infrequent and dangerous at best. Around the corner is Point Vicente Fishing Access, which has some very good kelp diving. White Point is the only place on Palos Verdes where you can actually drive your car to the water's edge. You'll find a lot of divers at White Point but it's still an enjoyable excursion. A little over a half-mile down the road is shore access on the west side of Point Fermin, but the water here is quite dirty. Cabrillo Beach near Los Angeles Harbor has good access but, again, poor water visibility. The harbor prevents any diving until you reach the sandy beaches of Orange County.

To experience rare sights like this spectacular purple gorgonian, you need to dive often and in the right places. Most areas in Los Angeles County will yield memorable experiences. ➤

Typical depth range	: 20–45 feet
Access	: Stairway to sandy cove; beach
Water entry	: Surf entry from sandy beach
Snorkeling	: Good

One of the largest kelp beds along the Southern California coast lies just 20 yards off Leo Carillo State Beach. The shoreline runs east to west, with two sandy beaches separated by the rocky Sequit Point. A giant kelp forest anchors itself to the rocky reef with pencil-thin strands that form the holdfast. Clusters of fronds spread in dense tangles, supporting a large population of marine life including urchins, starfish, anemones, nudibranchs, mollusks, and small sponges. Photographers should explore the rocks under the kelp beds for the best photos of marine creatures, and don't forget to look on the outer edges of the reefs for colorful gorgonians.

Hunters will find a few small lobster, abalone, and rock scallops concealed under the rocks. The kelp beds also shelter a wide variety of game fish, including kelp bass and sheepshead. Halibut can be spotted on the sand between the reefs.

Among the rocks and crevices at Leo Carillo State Beach, divers come across an array of intertebrates and marine life.

Feather-duster worms will pull back into their hole if disturbed. Approach quietly to observe their full splendor.

You can access the beach to the west of the point but, during the winter months, a storm can sometimes wash out the road that leads to the beach. Recently, brush fires have damaged some of the facilities here. There is a good side to the winter storms; the road closure keeps the crowds away. If the road is open, there is a fee for day use and camping.

Your best bet is to park on the seaward side of the highway near the "Mulholland Highway" sign. It's just a short walk down a gentle slope to the entry-exit areas on the point. Immediately to the west of lifeguard tower #2 and to the east of tower #3 is a stairway that leads to sandy coves located between the rocks. These are good areas for entries and exits. The enormous kelp bed starts about 20 yards from shore and extends a quarter-mile out. Rips and currents can be unpredictable, so observe conditions carefully. Lifeguards work during the summer and on some holidays; it's best to check water conditions with them before getting wet.

There are some rocks in the surf, but these shouldn't pose a problem as long as you note their position before entry. The bottom drops off moderately. Although the kelp is abundant, in most locations it's not thick enough to obstruct underwater passage. On the bottom, the reefs rise 10 feet in some spots. An occasional tall boulder can be found covered with feather worms, anemones, and other interesting invertebrates.

The diving area at Leo Carillo is large. You can enter the water from the beaches on either side of the point. Despite their close proximity, each beach offers a different experience to divers. It would take several dives just to begin exploring the special attractions of the area.

Typical depth range	: 10–40 feet
Access	: Dirt path, stairway
Water entry	: Surf entry from sandy beach
Snorkeling	: Fair

Four beaches to the south of Leo Carillo—Nicolas Canyon (not a state beach), El Pescador, La Piedra, and El Matador—offer good diving without the crowds that congregate at Leo Carillo. El Matador Beach is the southernmost beach in this string of state beaches. El Matador is located off Pacific Coast Highway (Highway 1), approximately four miles south of Leo Carillo and two miles north of Transcas Beach. You'll find ample parking, restrooms, and picnic tables. The park is open from 8 a.m. to sunset; no overnight camping is allowed. There is a day-use fee which you pay at a self-service box located on the side wall of the outdoor toilets. There's no running water.

A moderately steep path leads to the beach. The path is broken up by two sections of stairs, which together amount to about 80 steps. Before descending the steps, take a few minutes to take in the beauty of the beach. Almost directly off the beach is a reef with rocks that break the surface. The reef extends out about 75 yards in depths of between 10–20 feet. Although kelp grows here, visibility can be reduced by surge. Snorkeling is also good when the surf is low. Looking out past the shallow reefs, you'll see another kelp bed 75–150 yards out. These reefs offer the best

El Matador Beach is rugged, yet beautiful. The long reef system is made up mostly of large boulders.

Most of the reefs at El Matador Beach consist of very large boulders on a sandy, rocky bottom. This site offers an ample variety of color and marine life to pique anyone's interest.

diving, with depths ranging from 25–35 feet. Large kelp beds extending along the shoreline in both directions create a huge diving area that will satisfy divers at all skill levels.

Most of the reefs consist of very large boulders on a sandy, rocky bottom. Some boulders rise 15 feet from the bottom, displaying clusters of gorgonian, corynactis, and giant keyhole limpets. While there are other sites in Southern California better suited to macrophotography and sightseeing, El Matador offers ample variety of color and marine life to pique anyone's interest. Watch for the Garibaldi, senoritas, and even a few bluebanded gobies darting about.

Underwater hunters will find sheepshead, rockfish, and kelp bass. Halibut can sometimes be seen on the sand surrounding the reefs. Although the game fish in this area aren't particularly large, the quantity is sufficient. Among the selection are lobster and a limited number of abalone. Scallops can also be found.

Conditions at El Matador vary because the beach is exposed to weather. A day or two of pounding surf or rain can reduce visibility considerably. On good days, visibility averages 10–15 feet, though it can reach 30 feet on calm winter days or when the Santa Ana winds kick up. Currents don't pose much of a problem and usually only affect the outer edges of the kelp beds.

Typical depth range	: 30–80 feet
Access	: Stairway; sandy beach
Water entry	: Sandy beach
Snorkeling	: Poor

Around the turn of the century, Redondo Beach was the hub of Los Angeles' maritime trade. Redondo Canyon, a deep offshore submarine canyon, enabled merchant ships to come in close to shore when the seas were calm. In the late 19th Century, piers were erected off the beach to service the growing merchant trade. The area quickly became a popular vacation spot for residents of nearby Los Angeles, who could be seen strolling the piers or watching ships bringing cargo from the Northwest and Far East pull into port.

In time, three piers were built. Pier #1 stood at the foot of Emerald Street. It was destroyed in 1914 by a violent storm, but has since been

The macrophotography lens captures a tiny hermit crab perched on a reef. An abundance of marine life can be found among the pilings and canyon walls near the Redondo piers. Photograph by Len Tillim.

rebuilt into the famous "Horseshoe Pier." Pier #2 was a Y-shaped pier located at Ainsworth Court, next to Veteran's Park (then the luxurious Redondo Hotel). It, too, was heavily damaged by a storm in 1915 and was eventually torn down. The 480-foot Pier #3, located at Sapphire Street, met a similar fate in 1926. By time, the shipping boom at Redondo Beach

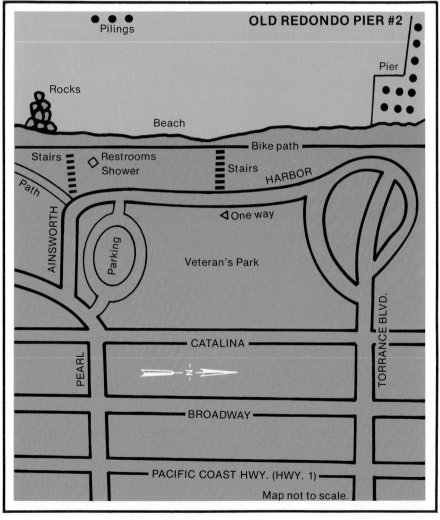

Historic Redondo Beach in Los Angeles is the site of late 19th century piers built to service merchant ships. Some of the piers were destroyed by storms, and they are now considered to be spectacular dive sites.

was nearing an end, as a new port was being constructed at San Pedro. Redondo Harbor is beyond the present-day pier. Since boat traffic can be busy at times, a flag and float is recommended.

All that remains of Pier #2 are three broken pilings, located just beyond the lip of the canyon less than 80 yards from shore in 45 feet of water. All are within 10 feet of each other and lie parallel to the shore and canyon. Colorful anemones adorn the pilings and tiny shrimp and an occasional octopus can also be seen nearby. From the pilings, the canyon drops rapidly to about 70 feet and then moderately to greater depths. To the north, the canyon walls are slightly steeper and drop to as much as 90 feet before tapering off. Stay well to the south of the existing pier, because it's illegal to dive on or near the pier.

Although the canyon isn't as spectacular as the La Jolla Canyon in San Diego, just to peer into the darkness from the edge can be an exhilarating experience. As you might expect, the water here is clear and cold. Visibility averages 15–20 feet, but during upwellings, visibility of 40 feet is possible.

An abundance of marine life can be found on the sandy and muddy bottom. At the edge of the canyon and along the canyon slope, sea pens poke from the sand and blue-gray spiny sand stars make their way across the bottom. In the canyon, you may see an octopus hiding in a discarded jar, crabs amidst the debris, and an occasional lobster crawling from the depths.

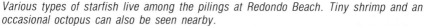

Various types of starfish live among the pilings at Redondo Beach. Tiny shrimp and an occasional octopus can also be seen nearby.

The shallow reefs of Picnic Beach provide spectacular underwater sightseeing.

To reach the park, head west on Torrance Boulevard. Turn left on Catalina Avenue. A parking lot is located at the intersection of Esplanade and Catalina, south of the Elk's Club and Veteran's Park. Turn right on Esplanade to get into the parking lot. There's plenty of metered parking to the south and west of Veteran's Park. Don't forget to bring plenty of quarters for the meter.

A stairway leading to the beach is located at the west end of the lot. Restrooms and showers are situated at the base of the stairs. Water entry is easy if the surf is low. Because of the canyon, surf is usually two feet lower than at other beaches nearby.

Typical depth range	: 30–50 feet
Access	: Stairway; sandy beach
Water entry	: Surf entry from sandy beach
Snorkeling	: Poor

The 460-foot Pier #3 off Sapphire Street was the busiest of the piers at Redondo Beach in the early 1900s. A railroad which carried cargo to and from the merchant ships ran to the end of the pier. There was also a restaurant owned by The Pacific Steamship Company at the end of the pier. While only three pilings remain of Pier #2, there are still many artifacts from Pier #3 to be found.

Among these artifacts are more than 20 pilings that rise as much as 12 feet from the bottom. The pilings are covered with beautiful pink anemones which make interesting photo subjects. You may also recover a few bricks and broken dishes from the restaurant. If you're lucky, you may even find a bottle or a dish bearing an insignia.

To reach the area, take Pacific Coast Highway (Highway 1) and turn west on either Sapphire or Topaz in Redondo Beach. Both of these streets end at the Esplanade. Park along the street and take the path between the buildings at both locations to get to the beach. Water entry is just north of the jetty. Facilities include showers and restrooms.

Water entry is generally easy in light to moderate surf. The sandy bottom slopes gently to approximately 35 feet about 100 yards from shore. This is where remnants of the pier pilings can first be spotted. To get to the pier, swim on the surface outward from the beach to just beyond the jetty. You should be directly out from the second set of condominiums situated north of the jetty. Many divers locate the wreckage by swimming north-

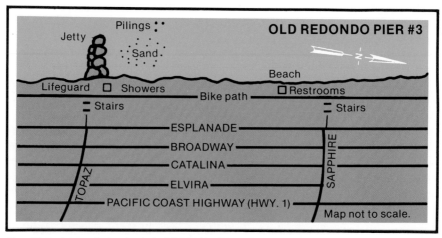

Pier #3 was one of the destroyed Redondo Beach Piers that serviced merchant ships at the turn of the century. The main attraction these days is the sunken pilings, now over-grown with sea life. On shore, facilities include restrooms and showers.

Turn-of-the-century artifacts like these have been taken over a long period from the sunken pier area.

west across the bottom at a 45 degree angle from the end of the jetty. Don't be discouraged if you miss the wreckage on first try. The pier area is long and narrow and it's very easy to swim too far north, south, or too close to shore.

Look for the bricks scattered on the bottom and you're in the area. Simply fan the bottom with your hand to uncover broken fragments of dishes. The broken pilings here are short and often covered with kelp. Depending on the weather, the kelp may reach the surface at some locations, indicating the location of the dive site.

The tall pilings are seaward and at the southern edge of Redondo canyon in about 40–45 feet of water. The canyon begins to drop off moderately north of here. If, in your search for pilings, you find yourself dropping into the canyon, you've gone too far to the north. Move up the sloping bottom and head south. The pilings are positioned about 15–25 feet apart so you have to move around to spot all of them. The outermost pilings are about 200 yards from shore.

Ocean conditions at this dive site are generally very good. Visibility averages 10–20 feet. Upwellings from nearby Redondo canyon can increase visibility to 30 feet. Surf is little or no problem, particularly during the summer months when the beach, which faces west, is well protected from the predominantly southerly swell. Prevailing westerlies during the winter can occasionally bring big surf, while currents are almost nonexistent. The only real hazard facing divers is the boat traffic from nearby Redondo Beach, so a flag and float are recommended.

Hunting in the area is generally limited to halibut, which are often taken in the sand surrounding the pilings. At times you can spot a small kelp bass. Sculpin and cabezon have been known to frequent the area. Other marine life include the comical and slow-moving sheep crab, octopus, sea pens, and sea pansies.

Typical depth range	: 10–30 feet
Access	: Paved path
Water entry	: Surf entry from sandy beach and rocks
Snorkeling	: Good

Malaga Cove lies where the long sweeping beaches of the Los Angeles South Bay end and the rocks and cliffs of Palos Verdes begin. This makes for an interesting bottom of sand, rocky reefs, and kelp beds. Lobster aren't uncommon in the rocky areas, but most aren't very big. Considering the good access to Malaga Cove, these waters hold a fair amount of game, including kelp bass (around the kelp beds) and halibut on the sand. For those who don't mind a long swim, you'll find rock scallops farther out.

For photographers and sightseers, diving Malaga Cove will show you marine life not common at other dive sites around Palos Verdes. Don't be surprised if you come across an angel shark buried in the sand. Some divers claim they've spotted angel sharks as long as five feet! Also look closely in the rocks for horn shark, octopus or sheep crab. These and other creatures—bat stars, ochre stars, nudibranchs, gorgonians, and Garibaldi—are also present.

To reach Malaga Cove, exit Pacific Coast Highway in Redondo Beach to Palos Verdes Boulevard south. You'll pass through a portion of Torrance before reaching Palos Verdes Estates. The road bears east before heading

Urchins are very popular along California's coast. They rest in crevices where they are sometimes hard to see. Their long spiny needles can penetrate even a wetsuit.

Garibaldi and a large variety of invertebrates and game fish share the reefs at Malaga Cove.

to the west, passing in front of the beautiful Malaga Cove Plaza. Turn right on Via Corta, which turns into Via Almar. Turn right at Via Arroyo in front of the Malaga Cove School. This will lead you to Paseo Del Mar. The parking lot will be on the right. After parking, proceed to the gazebo that overlooks the cove from the cliff above. From this vantage point you'll get a good indication of water conditions below.

A paved path leads to the beach. It's a moderately steep but short path. If you have a cart you can wheel your gear down to the beach and suit up there. There are two areas from which to enter the water. Where you enter will depend on personal preference and water and weather conditions. The first is from the rocks adjacent to and in front of the swimming pool. The second is from the beach. Entering from the rocks shortens the swim to the outer kelp beds considerably, but can be hazardous in moderate to heavy surf. The water immediately in front of the rocks is shallow. High tide is the best time to enter from the rocks. Many divers prefer to enter at the sandy beach and swim out to the edge of the reefs. But watch out for surfers here.

Although visibility averages 12 feet, conditions at the cove vary considerably. The cove is vulnerable to westerly and northwesterly swells. Under these conditions, it's recommended that you head to the other side of the peninsula. Runoff from rain can also affect visibility. Diving conditions are superb and visibility can reach 25 feet if winds are from the south or if the Santa Ana winds are blowing.

Sun worshippers should head to Torrance Beach (adjacent to the cove), where there are fewer crowds compared with other beaches on the South Bay.

Typical depth range	: 15–35 feet
Access	: Short, steep trail
Water entry	: Surf entry from rocks
Snorkeling	: Good

Haggerty's is named for a millionaire who used to live at this location. The diving here is very good, and while access can be difficult at times, it's not impossible.

Haggerty's is located less than one-half mile southwest of Malaga Cove. Follow Pacific Coast Highway to Torrance. Turn south on Palos Verdes Drive West and follow it to the city of Palos Verdes Estates. Across from Malaga Cove Plaza, turn right at Via Corta and head toward the sea. Continue down the hill where Via Corta turns into Via Almar. Turn right at the first stop sign onto Via Arroyo. You'll pass the Malaga Cove Elementary School. Turn left at the intersection of Via Arroyo and Paseo del Mar. After passing the Neighborhood Church on the right, park on the street at Via Chino. Across a small field, the path that leads to the beach begins at the top of the bluff.

The path is short and steep. Only the sure-footed should attempt the path. Take it slow, particularly on the lower section. Avoid this access if it has rained recently because the path becomes muddy and slippery. The top of the bluff offers an excellent vantage point from which to check out the surf, entry and exit points, and water conditions. Enter the water from

Turning over rocks will reveal a number of juvenile marine animals. This is a young sea bat starfish that, when fully grown, will reach up to six inches across.

the rocks. Should you find the path impassable, you may wish to dive Malaga Cove just down the road.

The bottom at Haggerty's is relatively flat and consists of rock and low-lying reefs that slope gently to 35 feet on the outer edges of the kelp. The kelp is thick in a few spots but not enough to obstruct passage. Perhaps the best thing about the kelp here is that it harbors one of the largest variety of marine life in the Palos Verdes area.

Huge sheep crabs are common on the reefs. It's not unusual to see three or four sheep crabs in one dive, some of which are two feet wide. Explore the kelp beds for sea hares—some are as large as a soccer ball—and clusters of yellow sea hare eggs.

Other sites in Palos Verdes are more colorful, but photographers will find plenty of subject matter here to keep the cameras clicking. The visibility is generally good and the plush kelp beds create a natural background. Visibility averages 15 feet. During the summer and fall, visibility on some days will reach 20–25 feet. By contrast, winter storms and rain tend to reduce visibility considerably. Currents are barely recognizable here, but surf can be a problem when the area is hit by westerly swells. The area is protected from southerly swells during the summer, creating good diving conditions.

Game fish are available in limited numbers. Both Malaga Cove and Haggerty's consistently produce lobster, though not in large numbers. A close look may reveal an abalone hiding under the rock ledges. Unlike the area between Palos Verdes Point and Dana Point, ab hunting is legal here. However, to protect the fish community, local divers have a "gentleman's agreement" not to take abalone north of Palos Verdes Point.

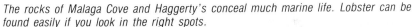
The rocks of Malaga Cove and Haggerty's conceal much marine life. Lobster can be found easily if you look in the right spots.

Typical depth range	:	25–40 feet
Access	:	Dirt path
Water entry	:	Surf entry from rocks
Snorkeling	:	Good

Many divers agree that the west side of Palos Verdes offers some of the best coastal diving in Southern California. However, many of the sites are difficult—if not impossible—to access. The exception is Flat Rock Point, located where the coastline at Palos Verdes swings to the south.

Here you'll find good diving on an interesting sea bottom. The bottom drops off quickly from shore to depths of 25–35 feet. The terrain consists mostly of boulders and reefs that run in ridges and rise 5–10 feet. Between the ridges, small patches of ivory sand create clearings in the thick kelp beds that blanket the area. The lush kelp and unusual reef formations support an excellent variety of marine life. Numerous Garibaldi, senoritas, kelp bass, sheepshead, and other varieties are present. There are few species of game fish,with the possible exception of large halibut that pass over the small sand patches between the reefs.

Hunters will no doubt delight in the large population of lobster here. Many of the reefs near the shoreline have been picked clean of the larger "bugs." A few can still be found in the shallows and even in very deep water. Abalone are slowly making a comeback,thanks to the efforts of local divers who've agreed not to hunt them here.

Nudibranchs, mollusks without shells or gills, are popular among California's southern coast, including the Los Angeles coastline.

Colorful marine life thrives in the reefs and ridges that make up Flat Rock. The kelp and unusual reef formations support an excellent variety of game fish and anemones.

Photographers and sightseers should enjoy the usually good visibility, which averages 15–20 feet. Colorful nudibranchs, starfish, gorgonians, and anemones make their home on the bottom. Other invertebrates, including an abundance of sea cucumbers, keyhole limpets, and sea hares, are also present. Look in the reef crevices for yellow and black striped treefish, small (and shy) bluebanded gobies, and an occasional horn shark. Urchins are common, so watch those knees!

Shore access to the point is difficult but not impossible. Flat Rock Point is located down the road from Haggerty's and Malaga Cove. Proceed to the area via Pacific Coast Highway. Once you reach the city of Torrance, exit to Palos Verdes Boulevard south. Follow this to the town of Palos Verdes Estates, past the Malaga Cove Plaza. Turn right on Via Corta, which turns into Via Almar as it bears to the left. After passing Via Arroyo, Via Aromitas, and Via Media, you'll come to Paseo Del Mar. Turn left. The head of the trail leading to Flat Rock Point will be directly ahead, where the road rises sharply and begins to curve to the left at 600 Paseo del Mar.

The trail to the beach begins as an old dirt road (sorry, no vehicles permitted). The trail breaks off to a moderately steep dirt path. Avoid the trail after a rain because the path can become muddy and very slippery. Even when dry, the trail can be treacherous, so proceed with caution.

The trail ends at the flat rocks on the point. Depending on the size and direction of the surf, entry is from the rock where depths drop sharply to 12 feet. Experience in this type of entry and exit is recommended. Under the right surf conditions, there are some small coves in the rocks to the northeast of the point that can also be used.

Typical depth range	:	10–50 feet
Access	:	Dirt path
Water entry	:	Surf entry from rocky beach
Snorkeling	:	Good

The reefs at Christmas Tree Cove are quite spectacular in some spots. In one location, a large section of the reef—the size of a bus—juts 18 feet from the bottom and drops vertically to a kelp bed below. Other areas of the reef are marked by overhangs, channels, and huge boulders. Lush kelp beds surround the reefs. Christmas Tree Cove has the best water visibility in the area. Averaging 15–25 feet, visibility rarely drops below 10 feet and can be as great as 35 feet.

The thick kelp and rugged bottom terrain inhabit a wide variety of sea life, including sponges, anemones, starfish, mollusks, the giant keyhole limpet, turban snail, kellet's whelk and brown chestnut cowrie. Red and blue Spanish shawl and bright yellow sea lemon nudibranchs provide interesting splashes of color here and there. You'll also see opaleye, rock wrasse, Garibaldi, and hundreds of senoritas swimming above and around the reefs. Look for the striped treefish in crevices and the tiny and colorful bluebanded goby darting about.

Brittle stars are common, but they are not always seen without looking carefully in cracks and crevices.

Christmas Tree Cove has poor shore access, but the clear waters and colorful sea life just outside the small bay make this a fantastic dive site.

Game fish are also plentiful, though not as abundant as in other areas off Palos Verdes. Halibut are sometimes found on the sand that surrounds the kelp, as are kelp bass, sheepshead, and a small population of rockfish. You may also find some scallops and lobster. Keep in mind that it's illegal to take abalone from the area.

The only drawback to this site is the poor shore access—a steep dirt path along the north side of the cove. Only the sure-footed diver should attempt this route. And exercise caution after a rain; the path can become slippery and muddy. To reach the path, take Pacific Coast Highway to Palos Verdes Drive West. Follow this road south for approximately five miles (you'll drive through the town of Palos Verdes Estates). Turn west on Paseo Lunado. The road turns into Paseo Del Mar as it swings along the coast. The foot of the path is located in the 2800 block of Paseo del Mar near the intersection of Paseo Del Mar and Via Neve. There's limited but ample street parking. There are no facilities.

Ocean conditions can be easily observed from the top of the bluff. After proceeding down the steep trail, water entry can be made through the surf at the stone and gravel beach in the center of the cove. Or, if conditions permit, you can enter from the rocks on either side of the cove. It's a long swim through thick kelp to reach the best reefs on the outer edges of the kelp. There are some interesting reefs and kelp beds closer to shore.

Typical depth range	:	20–50 feet
Access	:	Dirt path
Water entry	:	Surf entry from rocky beach
Snorkeling	:	Good

Local divers have come to accept the difficult shore access at many of the dive sites around Palos Verdes. Point Vicente, nicknamed "Cardiac Hill," is no exception. But it's really not as bad as it sounds. The steep trail is located to the west of the Point Vicente lighthouse—a stone's throw from Marineland. There's adequate parking. Restrooms and a drinking fountain are located at the top of the trail. "Cardiac Hill" is long and steep but fairly safe. Diving along the shoreline at the bottom of the hill is worth the effort.

The beach between Point Vicente and Long Point (where Marineland is located) is fairly large and offers a wide diving area. The best location is to the east, at the end of the branch of the trail that heads toward a small rocky point. The east branch trail is a little narrow in some spots but visibility is best here. And, depending on conditions, entries are easiest from this spot.

By contrast, entry over the rocks can sometimes be difficult. It's fairly easy to enter and exit from the sandy beach in the center of the cove. But this results in a long swim to reach the clearest waters to the east. Before

The tube anemone is usually orange in color, but its tentacles can be purple to black.

descending the trail, determine the conditions and your diving goals to choose the best entry/exit point and dive spot.

The bottom drops off gradually to 50 feet just 150 yards from shore, eventually leveling to a sandy bottom. Most of the reefs consist of boulders of varying sizes. Some are large and extend to within 10 feet of the surface, creating large caves and overhangs that are exciting to explore. If water visibility is good, you can sometimes spot these large boulders from the cliff top.

Visibility in this area is fair, averaging 10–15 feet. The best visibility is usually on the east side of the cove, which is somewhat protected from northwest swells but susceptible to southerly swells during the summer. The bottom is covered mostly with silt which can reduce visibility during heavy surf. Close to shore, strong currents aren't usually a problem, but near Point Vicente, currents have been known to reach two knots.

Marine life near the rocks is not as abundant as in other areas around Palos Verdes, but there is certainly enough variety for sightseers, photographers, and hunters. Expect to see giant keyhole limpets and nudibranchs and, on the ledges and overhangs, corynactis anemones. Numerous strands of gorgonians add color to the deeper waters. Sea hares and sea cucumbers are also common in deep waters. Fish life includes Garibaldi, senoritas, opaleye, and halibut. There are a few scallops and lobster as well. Kelp cover on the reefs is patchy. If the kelp growth is heavy you can expect more game moving in the cove. Hunting for abs is strictly prohibited here.

Strong currents at Point Vicente have no effect on the white-spotted rose anemone.

Typical depth range	:	To 45 feet
Access	:	Roadway
Water entry	:	Surf entry from rocky beach
Snorkeling	:	Good

White Point is the only location along the Palos Verdes Peninsula where you can drive right down to the water's edge. Thousands of divers have taken their first dive here and, although this location is considered a beginner's spot, divers of all skill levels will find something of interest.

Prior to World War II, the local Japanese-American community built a bathhouse here over natural hot water vents. Remains of this bathhouse are visible just above the high tide mark, but the hot water vents are only visible underwater. The vents are located on the rocky bottom close to shore (the nearest vent is less than 25 yards out). They're identified by the strange white fungus that surrounds them. You can actually feel the warm water rising from some of the larger vents. If your hands get cold while diving, simply run your fingers through the warm sand at the vents.

The blue banded goby is colorful, shy and seldom larger than 1½ inches. Although abundant in the Southern California waters, they are seldom seen. Any disturbance causes them to retreat into tiny crevices. Photograph by Len Tillim.

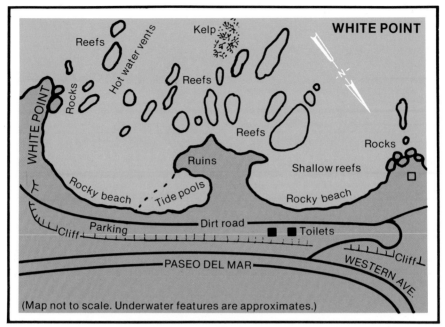

Beach access is as easy as driving your car onto the beach at White Point. Spectacular sights in this area include the ruins of a pre-World War II bathhouse on shore, and the hot water vents on the ocean bottom not far from shore.

Diving in the surrounding area is, quite frankly, not as spectacular and beautiful as in other areas along the peninsula. But there are some interesting features. The shallow waters offer plenty of scenery for the novice snorkeler. Beyond this area, there are reefs that extend off the points to the north and south, forming overhangs, crevices, and small caves. Approximately 150 yards out, three reefs run parallel to each other, separated by sandy patches. Here, in 35–45 feet of water, is the best diving around. The offshore reefs are, however, best left to more experienced divers who can handle the longer swim and currents.

Starfish (including the colorful bat star), ochre star, and many nudibranchs (particularly the beautiful orange and blue Spanish shawl,)can be found on the reefs. Other invertebrates here include a variety of anemones, sea cucumbers, giant keyhole limpets, and, in deeper waters, gorgonians. At one time there was an underwater nature trail, but heavy storms in recent years have destroyed it. There are plans to rebuild it.

For the photographer there are also some morays, but surprisingly few Garibaldi. Fish populations have been depleted over the years, but some species are making a comeback. Lobster can be found on reefs located in deep water. Abalone, particularly black abalone, are making a slow comeback, *but hunting abalone is prohibited.* Sheepshead, halibut, and kelp bass are available on the deeper reefs, while perch and opaleye reside in shallow waters.

The black-eyed goby is very common along most of the Southern California coastline.

Years ago, a ship wrecked on the point and broke up. Subsequent storms broke the ship into tiny pieces and spread them over a wide area. Look closely for brass nails and other small items.

Conditions at White Point are usually good. Visibility on the reefs averages 10–15 feet. Conditions on the deeper offshore reefs can be somewhat better. The small cove where most divers enter is protected from weather most of the time, but conditions can be hazardous on the rocks at high tide.

To reach White Point and nearby Royal Palms State Beach, proceed south along Western Avenue through the town of San Pedro. The road will swing to the left and join with Paseo Del Mar. The road to the point is located less than one block away at 1800 W. Paseo Del Mar. It's the only road that leads to the water and, though unmarked, it's hard to miss. There is sometimes a $3 day use fee for the state park (Royal Palms), depending on the time of year and time of day. Proceed down the hill and bear left until the road turns to dirt. A small cove is approximately 100 feet ahead. Park on the side of the road. Most divers enter from the cove, which is just a few steps from the water's edge. Some divers prefer to enter off the rocks at either point, but this is recommended only for experienced divers. In the cove, enter the water from the rocks.

California golden gorgonian is common in areas off Los Angeles County.

Diving in Orange County

The coastline of Orange County offers the heaviest concentration of beach diving sites in Southern California. From the Los Angeles County line to the southern side of the mouth of Newport Harbor, diving is generally limited to sandy bottoms or under piers where permitted. Just south of the mouth of Newport Harbor is the beach at Corona del Mar. You can dive on the shallow rocks to the south, or on the Newport Harbor breakwater. The small cove at Little Corona, the next beach down the coast, is flanked on both sides by interesting rocky reefs. Past the town of Corona Del Mar is Crystal Cove State Beach. Having recently undergone extensive renovation, the facilities here are excellent. There are several good shore access points in the park, but the one that leads to the best diving is at Scotchman's Cove (Reef Point).

Heading southward into the town of Laguna Beach are a number of beach diving spots. You'll find good diving at Crescent Bay, but the best diving is a very long swim offshore to Deadman's Reef. Nearby Shaw's Cove is usually very crowded but offers good diving. Equally spectacular (and much less crowded) is the diving off the small Fisherman's Cove. Most of the divers who start off at nearby Diver's Cove usually end up on the reef at Fisherman's Cove. From Diver's Cove, the coast flattens out into a small sandy beach known as Picnic Beach. Here you'll find excellent facilities and good, easy diving in the kelp offshore. Picnic Beach shares its facilities with Rocky Beach, but entries here are a bit more difficult. Once you get over the rocks, though, the diving here is often better than at Picnic Beach.

Reefs thin out and hang farther offshore as you approach the Main Beach near downtown Laguna Beach. There is good beach access at Cleo and Cress Streets, but these beaches are exposed to weather, and it's a long swim to the reefs. Small coves, such as Woods Cove or the one at Moss Street, are more protected from the weather and offer excellent reef formations close to shore.

Orange County is known for its good beach diving. Facilities in the diving areas of Orange County are usually well-equipped, and water entries are generally safe and easy. Dive sites include: Little Corona (17), Scotchman's Cove (18), Shaw's Cove (19), Fisherman's Cove (20), Picnic Beach (21), Rocky Beach (22), Wood's Cove (23), and Moss Street (24). ➤

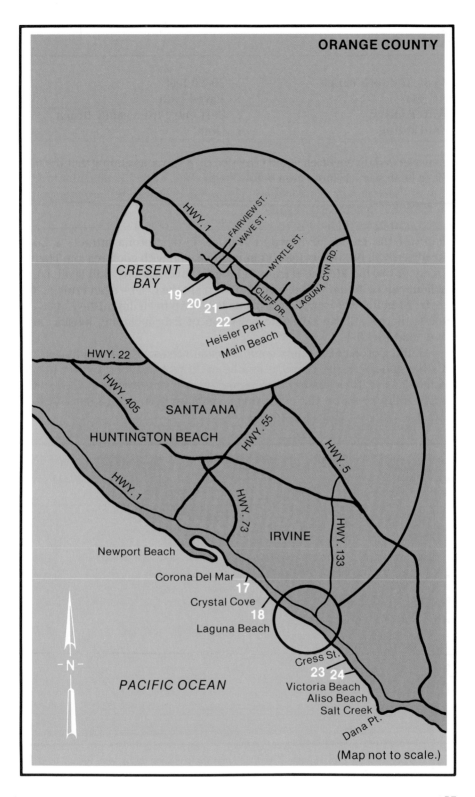

ORANGE COUNTY

CRESENT BAY

HWY. 1

FAIRVIEW ST.
WAVE ST.
MYRTLE ST.
LAGUNA CYN. RD.
CLIFF DR.

19
20 21
22
Heisler Park
Main Beach

HWY. 22

HWY. 405

SANTA ANA

HUNTINGTON BEACH

HWY. 55

HWY. 5

HWY. 1

HWY. 73

IRVINE

HWY. 133

Newport Beach

Corona Del Mar

17
Crystal Cove

18
Laguna Beach

Cress St.

23 24
Victoria Beach
Aliso Beach
Salt Creek

Dana Pt.

-N-

PACIFIC OCEAN

(Map not to scale.)

Typical depth range	:	20–30 feet
Access	:	Paved path
Water entry	:	Surf entry from sandy beach
Snorkeling	:	Good

Experienced divers often avoid crowded dive spots, assuming that the best dives lie in some remote area below steep cliffs. Little Corona, however, is one of those popular spots where, if you can deal with the crowds, you're in for some spectacular diving.

Located in the southern corner of Newport Beach less than a mile south of the mouth of Newport Harbor, Little Corona attracts a fairly steady crowd. But divers keep coming back, and with good reason. There's plenty of marine life and terrain to interest divers at any skill level. Large halibut can be found in the sand and horn sharks can be seen cruising the reefs. Although the supplies of game fish have been diminished over the years, there's still an adequate selection of fish, including lobster, kelp bass, and rockfish.

Little Corona also offers some unusual scenery for the sightseer and photographer. On the reefs, in depths of 20 feet or more, expect to find gorgonians, starfish, feather worms, and other invertebrates. Visibility here is generally good; on the outer reefs, visibility averages 15 feet—30 feet

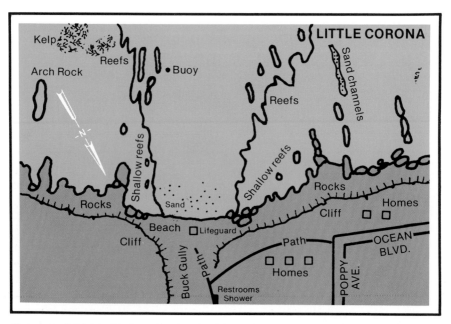

Divers should not let the crowded beach of Little Corona keep them from diving this area. A great deal of various marine life thrives among the reefs offshore.

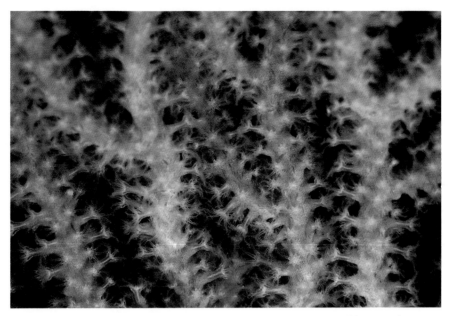

A close look reveals that many California marine creatures, such as this gorgonian, are made up of complex and simple patterns. Expect to find excellent photographic subjects and good visibility at Little Corona.

under the best conditions. Closer to shore, visibility can be reduced due to water turbulence over the sand, but it's usually good enough over the shallow reefs in calm weather for snorkeling.

The reefs start in shallow water and, approximately 150 yards out, slope down to 30 feet. Some of the shallow reefs are covered by a thick blanket of eel grass. The middle of the cove is mostly sand, but there are numerous small rocks in the surf line that can trip you up during entry and exit. The reefs lie on either side of the sandy cove. The most interesting reefs are located to the south about 100 yards out. A buoy in this area directs boats to stay clear. Other intriguing reefs lie just seaward and to the south of this buoy. Further down the coast is the unusual Arch Rock that rises from the water and usually hosts several species of birds. Despite the buoy directing boats to stay clear, the area is very close to Newport Harbor. For this reason, it is recommended that you use a flag and float.

Also keep in mind that this area is part of the Newport Beach Marine Life Refuge. It's illegal to remove any marine life other than normal game.

Little Corona can be reached by turning south onto narrow Poppy Street off East Coast Highway (Highway 1) in Newport Beach. Poppy Street deadends at a point that overlooks the sea, then turns sharply onto Ocean Boulevard. There's limited free parking on Ocean Boulevard. The path to Little Corona is to the left of this intersection. A moderately steep paved path winds down to the beach. Restrooms and showers are located halfway down the path, tucked in a corner to the left.

Scotchman's Cove (Reef Point)   18

Typical depth range	: 10–45 feet
Access	: Dirt path; stairway
Water entry	: Surf entry from sandy beach
Snorkeling	: Good

In the short history of sport diving, Scotchman's Cove has earned a solid reputation for its superb game fish population. Although the supply of game fish has diminished over the years, many beach divers still consider Scotchman's Cove a reliable hunting area. You'll discover lobster at depths of 30 feet and sometimes in the shallows among the eel grass. Scallops are also available, but usually in outer waters. Abalone are present in small numbers but it's illegal to take them. The most abundant species include calico, kelp bass, and sheepshead. Other fish can be found, but the heavy spearfishing activity in this area have scared off many species of fish.

Scotchman's Cove is also a good spot for underwater photography and sightseeing. The bottom drops off quickly to 10–20 feet. Several shallow reefs covered with eel grass make this an excellent area for snorkeling during calm weather. The deeper and more intriguing reefs lie 100–200 yards out. For the best sightseeing and game fish, stay close to the exposed offshore reef. In addition, there are large reef formations rising 20 feet from the bottom in some spots. These create immense walls of rock on which you'll see gorgonians, starfish, and anemones. There are plenty of crevices, cracks, and overhangs to explore, as well as the patches of sand that separate the reefs. Ribbon kelp grows from the rocks. Most of the larger kelp beds are gone, but may grow back in the near future.

This colorful, young female sheepshead makes a good photo subject. Be prepared to also see a large number of calico and kelp bass at Scotchman's Cove.

For the best sightseeing at Scotchman's Cove, stay close to the exposed offshore reef. There are large reef formations rising 20 feet from the bottom in some spots, and in the cracks and crevices, much colorful life thrives.

Visibility is generally good, averaging 10–15 feet. During the winter months, visibility can reach 20–30 feet. The area is open to heavy surf, which can reduce visibility when large swells roll in. But perhaps the most salient features of the area are the excellent facilities that have been installed recently on the bluff overlooking the beach. Scotchman's Cove lies at the southern end of Crystal Cove State Park. Many of the park's facilities have recently undergone renovation. New restrooms and fresh-water showers and sinks have been installed. Several new paved parking spaces have also been added. An underwater nature trail is planned for the near future. Because the cove lies within park boundaries, there's a $3 entrance fee charged at the gate.

To reach Scotchman's Cove, take Highway 1 to Laguna Beach. Follow the signs marked "Reef Point" to get to the gate. The path and stairs that lead to the beach are located just beyond the new restrooms on the bluff. The path is moderately steep but safe. You can get a bird's eye view of the diving area from the bluff. A large reef that extends from the point is located up the coast and to the right. Diving is good on both sides of the reef but, as always, weather, surf, and currents will determine the best diving area. Entry from the sandy beach is through surf. Keep in mind that the area is open to swells and should be avoided during periods of heavy surf.

Typical depth range	:	20–50 feet
Access	:	Stairway; path
Water entry	:	Surf entry from sandy beach or from rocks on point
Snorkeling	:	Good

Welcome to one of the most popular dive spots in Laguna Beach. Nearly every weekend it's not uncommon to see two or three classes using the cove for checkout dives. And don't be surprised if you see several buddy teams emerge from the water with smiles on their faces. Beach diving conditions here are as close to ideal as you're going to get along Laguna Beach. The crowds are perhaps the only drawback to the area, but don't let them turn you away from an otherwise superb dive site.

The cove is well protected from wave action. Consequently, the surf averages less than two feet. Currents are weak or nonexistent and the visibility is rarely below 15 feet. In fact, it often exceeds 35 feet.

Given these conditions, it's no wonder the cove is popular with diving instructors. Students can learn surf and rock entries and exits under mild conditions, and excellent snorkeling is also available.

The bottom terrain is both interesting and varied. On the western side of the cove, the rocks extend out from the point and drop rapidly to the sand in 20–35 feet of water. A 15-foot channel at the end of the point starts at 20 feet and cuts deep into the reef. To locate the "crevice," as it's called by local divers, swim seaward on the bottom along the edge of the rocks. The crevice begins as a 15-foot cut into the reef and extends to the west. The crevice then narrows to a tunnel that's filled with Garibaldi and other marine life. Eventually the crevice branches off into smaller channels and tunnels, where you'll find octopus that can be hand fed. A note of caution: The crevice is affected by surge and strong currents. Experienced divers will benefit from these conditions, as the surge helps direct visitors in and out of the channels. Underwater activities can be observed from the rocks at the surface directly above the crevice at low tide. Farther out along this reef in deeper water, gorgonians can be found attached to the rocks. Friendly Garibaldi are more abundant here. Nudibranchs and a variety of anemones add color to the area.

Game fish are sparse in Shaw's Cove, probably because of the number of divers who come here. Expect to find an occasional morsel on the outer fringes of the reef. You can take most game fish in the area but, because Shaw's Cove is part of the Laguna Beach Marine Life Refuge, there are some restrictions. Be familiar with the hunting regulations before you dive.

Diving on the eastern side of the cove is less spectacular but far less crowded. A shallow reef covered with blade kelp and eelgrass extends out

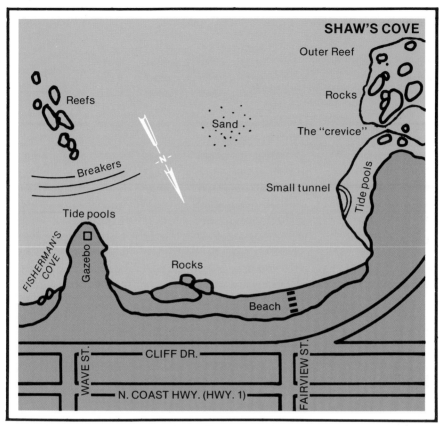

A very popular dive site, Shaw's Cove offers near-perfect diving conditions and average visibility. Divers of all abilities enjoy this spot because of the varied terrain and sea life.

approximately 100 yards from the eastern point. At several places the reef rises 8 feet above the bottom. Gorgonians and anemones cover the walls here. On the far side of the eastern reef, there's a shallow channel filled with a variety of fish and, in one particular crevice, two huge moray eels.

Shaw's Cove is located between two other favorite Laguna Beach dive sites—Crescent Bay to the north and Fisherman's Cove to the south. A short walkway and stairway leading to the cove are located at the end of Fairview at Cliff Drive, a block from the North Coast Highway (Highway 1). Street parking is limited, so it's best to arrive early on the weekends. If your schedule permits, you can miss the crowds by visiting Shaw's Cove during the week. Be aware that the area surrounding the cove is privately owned. Trespassers are discouraged!

As for facilities, there's a dive store located a block south of Fairview at the intersection of Wave Street and Highway 1. A burger stand is located across the street from the dive store.

Typical depth range	:	To 40 feet
Access	:	Short path
Water entry	:	Surf entry from sandy beach
Snorkeling	:	Good

Fisherman's Cove, also known as Boat Canyon, falls within the Laguna Beach Marine Life Refuge. While there are some restrictions on the type of game that can be hunted, there are no restrictions on the most popular catch—lobster. And because the area isn't as well known as other sites nearby, game fish continue to be in good supply. In addition to lobster (found in the cracks and crevices), sheepshead, kelp bass, and halibut abound. The lucky diver may even find a large scallop or two on the rocks. Keep in mind that the reef on the southeast end of Fisherman's Cove extends into Diver's Cove, which is part of a marine/ecological preserve. It's illegal to hunt in this area. The boundary is marked by a crack in the point which divides Diver's Cove and Fisherman's Cove (known as "Giggle Crack" by the locals). To play it safe, stay well northwest of the point and enter and exit only at Fisherman's Cove if you're hunting.

Besides game fish, you'll also find some interesting reef formations— some of the best in Laguna Beach. One such reef is located about 75 yards off the small beach. Rocks can be seen from the surface of this reef, which extends shoreward to the southeast side of the cove. The reef rises from a sandy bottom and offers a number of deep channels, large crevices, and overhangs to explore. The channel is located in 25 feet of water less than 60 yards from shore on the north edge of the reef. The channel varies in width from 10–20 feet, with walls that are 15 feet high. Farther out on the reef, the rock walls become quite steep, rising as much as 25 feet from the bottom. A few feet to the north, across the sand, are some medium-size patch reefs. You'll find more channels and crevices on the seaward side of the reef and to the east.

For the sightseer and photographer, there are gorgonians on the reef, some kelp, a sizeable population of Garibaldis, senoritas, kelpfish, opaleyes, octopusses, nudibranchs, and an occasional moray eel. Diving conditions here are as good as those at Shaw's and Diver's Coves and, unlike neighboring areas, Fisherman's Cove is somewhat protected from the southerly swells. Diving on the north side of the reef offers some protection from surge generated by the southerly swells. Visibility averages 15–20 feet. Strong currents are unusual and generally affect the outer reefs.

To reach Fisherman's Cove, drive to Laguna Beach on Highway 1 and exit toward the beach at Cliff Drive, located one block south of the dive store. Follow Cliff Drive as it bears to the left. The stairway and path leading to Fisherman's Cove are located to the right of the Laguna Sea Cliff Condominiums/Apartments. Park on the street or in the metered spots in front of Diver's Cove. Showers and restrooms are located at Heisler Park,

Fisherman's Cove is also called Boat Canyon because of the large number of boats stored ashore.

about 300 feet south of Diver's Cove. The beach is small and sometimes totally covered during high tide. Respect the privacy of residents.

Make your entry north of the reef. On the south side, between the outer rocks and the point, the reef comes very close to the surface, creating hazardous surf. North of the main reef is a sandy area and a shallow reef covered with eel grass. Within 20 feet of the shore, the bottom drops off quickly to 10 feet. To the north are shallow reefs that join up with the south end of Shaw's Cove. Some game fish and a wide variety of marine life can be found here. In the middle of this reef, in about 20 feet of water, is a wide crevice where two very large morays have been known to hide.

Typical depth range	: To 40 feet
Access	: Paved path
Water entry	: Surf entry from sandy beach
Snorkeling	: Good

The name of this dive spot suggests activities besides good diving. Be sure to pack a picnic lunch to enjoy between dives in the lush park on the bluff overlooking the beach. Restrooms, picnic tables, outdoor barbeques, and a freshwater shower are available.

Just off the wide and generally uncrowded beach a series of reefs stretch seaward more than 100 yards to depths of 40 feet or more. The reefs consist of a series of ridges that rise 10 feet from the sandy bottom. As you might expect, there are cracks, crevices, and overhangs to explore. In one spot there's a tunnel—too narrow for divers—that runs underneath a 20-foot reef. On your journey you'll see Garibaldis, senoritas, opaleyes,

Corynactis anemones provide one of the many splashes of color that grace Picnic Beach. They are small, seldom larger than 1/2-inch across, but they grow in large groups.

A diver examines a horn shark egg case. Marine life such as octopus, shrimp and lobster are available.

and bluebanded gobies. Colorful anemones, giant keyhole limpets, gorgonians, moon sponges, and Spanish shawl nudibranchs on the rocks provide perfect scenery for sightseers and photographers. The kelp beds on the reef are plush but not too dense to obstruct passage.

Picnic Beach is located in a marine preserve. Consequently, hunters are not welcome and sightseers should take nothing but pictures. Visibility averages 15–20 feet; during the winter months, visibility can reach 40 feet.

The area is located south of Diver's Cove. Take Highway 1 to Myrtle. Myrtle ends at Cliff Drive. Metered parking is available along Cliff Drive. The fee is 25 cents per half hour, so bring plenty of quarters. Crowds can be a problem during the summer, so arrive early. The ramp to the beach is slightly to the right and through the park. The cove is somewhat protected, so entry is usually easy. Avoid the center of the beach as there are rocks in the surf that break surface at low tide. Kelp is sparse on the reef that lies close to shore in 25–35 feet of water. The thicker kelp to the south is more easily reached by entering at nearby Rocky Beach.

Typical depth range	:	15–50 feet
Access	:	Stairway
Water entry	:	Surf entry from rocky beach
Snorkeling	:	Good

The shoreline at Rocky Beach is varied, offering a number of entry and exit points. A huge kelp bed extends from 50–200 yards offshore. In the middle of this—approximately 100 yards from shore—a large reef breaks the surface at low tide. A number of smaller reefs surround the large one, creating a huge diving area that can accommodate a good crowd of divers without making anyone feel claustrophobic.

A wide selection of entry and exit points doesn't imply that entry is easy. The diver should have some experience with surf entries over rocks. Entries and exits will be somewhat easier if the surf is light or moderate.

Close to shore, the bottom drops quickly to 10–15 feet. There are many small low-lying reefs, sand patches, and channels. The shallow reefs are excellent for snorkeling when the surf is low, but diving with tanks

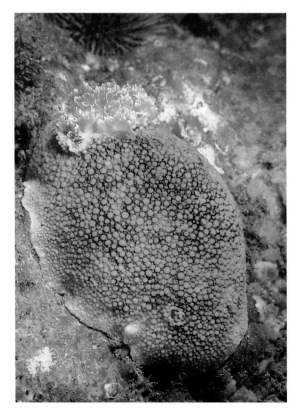

Although not as common as other nudibranchs, the sea lemon is occasionally found in areas off Southern California's coastline.

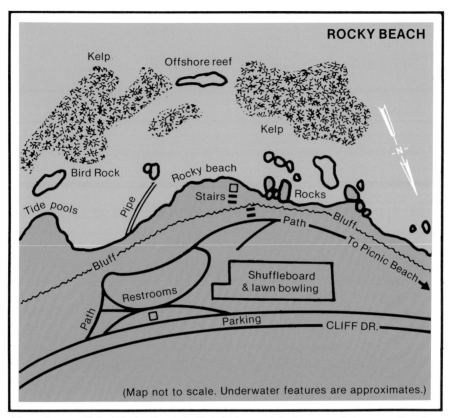

ROCKY BEACH

Kelp

Offshore reef

Kelp

Bird Rock

Rocky beach

Tide pools

Pipe

Stairs

Rocks

Path

Bluff

To Picnic Beach

Bluff

Path

Restrooms

Shuffleboard & lawn bowling

Parking

CLIFF DR.

(Map not to scale. Underwater features are approximates.)

Many divers will find Rocky Beach to their liking, mainly because of the versatility of the area. There are many entry/exit points, and a large kelp bed lies within 200 yards of shore. The area is large enough so that divers won't feel crowded, and the site is easy to find.

here can be difficult in moderate surf because of the surge. If you're using tanks, there's no reason to linger in the shallows because deeper water is just a short swim away. The larger reefs, particularly the one that breaks the surface at low tide, can be quite spectacular. At 20–30 feet, the reef walls drop vertically and then slope to depths of 40–50 feet. Kelp surrounds most of the area. Crabs, large anemones, and broad strands of gorgonians populate the rocks. Photographers will be happy to learn that the Garibaldis and senoritas are very cooperative. Expect to see horn sharks and yellowtails as well.

Game fish include lobster, halibut, and scallops, but *do not touch*! The area is a marine preserve, attracting a variety of creatures that aren't found elsewhere along the coast.

Rocky Beach is located south of Diver's Cove and Picnic Beach. Take Highway 1 through Laguna Beach. North of the center of town, turn onto Jasmine Street. There's metered parking along Cliff Drive. Two sets of stairs leading to the water's edge are located behind the shuffleboard and lawn bowling courts. Facilities at Heisler Park include showers, restrooms, and picnic areas.

Typical depth range	:	10–40 feet
Access	:	Path, stairway
Water entry	:	Surf entry from sandy beach
Snorkeling	:	Good

It's not unusual to see several hundred divers converge on the beaches in southern Orange County during the summer, particularly on weekends. To escape this madness, come to Woods Cove. This spectacular dive site offers all the qualities you would expect to find in a Laguna Beach dive spot, without the crowds. It's located at the southern end of Laguna Beach about two miles down the coast from Diver's Cove and Shaw's Cove. Perhaps the most salient feature of Wood's Cove is its interesting bottom terrain. Two main reefs dominate the bottom. To the east, starting approximately 50 yards out is a reef made up of jumbled boulders and rock outcroppings. Water depths average 30–40 feet about 100 yards out and the reef reaches to within 15 feet to the surface in some spots. To the west there's a low-lying reef in 30 feet of water covered with kelp that sports an interesting feature: a huge boulder that rises to within a

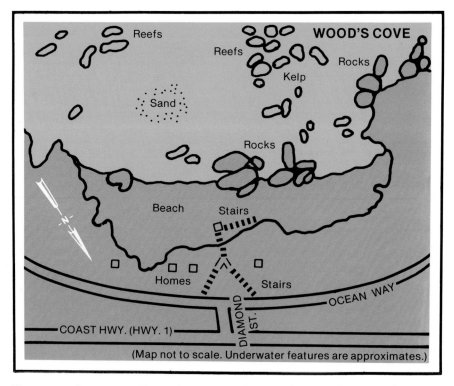

(Map not to scale. Underwater features are approximates.)

When many divers are rushing to join the crowds on the beaches of southern Orange County, others enjoy the solitude at Woods Cove, a less-frequented site that offers a wide variety of diving pleasures.

An area of Wood's Cove is covered in kelp. Don't miss the huge boulder around the kelp beds. It is an interesting spot to explore.

few feet of the surface. Take the opportunity to explore the overhangs created by boulder.

There are other wonders in the area. On the east side of the cove, friendly Garibaldi will feed from your hands. There's also a colorful array of invertebrates on the rocks, including nudibranchs, anemones, gorgonians, and starfish, and, on the western reef, a small kelp forest. Unlike neighboring sites, Wood's Cove is not part of a marine reserve. Hunting is permitted as long as you follow California Fish and Game regulations. However, it's illegal to take abalone here. The lobster population is sparse except perhaps in the shallows. Small numbers of scallops are also present. Look on the outer reefs for kelp bass and sheepshead, and on the sand between the reefs for halibut.

To reach Wood's Cove, exit Highway 1 on Diamond Street. The stairs leading to the beach and cove are located at the intersection of Diamond and Ocean Way. There's limited parking along both roads. The stairway cuts through a garden separating private property, so please be considerate. The sandy beach on the cove is divided by a large boulder. The best spot to enter is to the left of the boulder on the east side of the cove. Beware of submerged rocks that break the surface at low tide. During the summer, a southerly swell can create difficult diving conditions.

Typical depth range	:	To 35 feet
Access	:	Stairway
Water entry	:	Surf entry from sandy beach
Snorkeling	:	Good

The cove at Moss Street offers diving pleasures that rival other locations in Laguna Beach—without the crowds. There are small walls and ledges to explore, rocks that tower 18 feet from the sandy bottom, and deep crevices that cut into the reef to form small caves. Conditions here are generally good all year. The cove is well protected, and currents usually affect only the extreme outer reef. Visibility averages 15–25 feet and can reach 35 feet under ideal conditions. Shallow parts of the reef are sometimes affected by surge. Avoid this area by moving to deeper waters 30–35 feet on the reef located 100–150 yards offshore.

Moss Street is located off Highway 1, approximately one mile south of the downtown area. Limited parking is available on Moss Street and nearby Ocean Way. If there are no parking spots, simply drop your gear at the top of the stairs and park a few blocks away. Be aware of the "No Parking" zones—they're everywhere! A short stairway leads to the small sandy beach. You can plan your dive from the top of the stairs. Note the rocks that break the surface on the south and northwest sides of the cove (at low tide). The rocks at the southern point, known as Moss Point, mark

The horned nudibranch is more common up north, but it has been found occasionally at the Moss Street Reef.

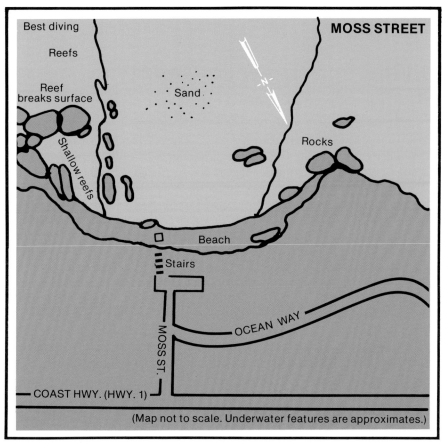

Best diving

Reefs

Reef
breaks surface

Shallow reefs

Sand

MOSS STREET

N

Rocks

Beach

Stairs

OCEAN WAY

MOSS ST.

COAST HWY. (HWY. 1)

(Map not to scale. Underwater features are approximates.)

Moss Street is another less-frequented Laguna Beach dive site. Divers who enjoy walls and ledges, hunters, and photographers will find this spot extraordinary.

the beginning of the reef that interests most divers. There are reefs on the northwest side of the cove, but they're flat and lack the variety of marine life of the main reef.

Upon entering, the bottom drops 5–6 feet. Beware of loose stones in the surf. The shallow water close to the beach is perfect for snorkeling on very calm days. To get to the southern reef, stay to your left as you face the ocean. You can avoid most of the surge by dropping to the bottom just beyond the rocks that break the surface. Beyond these rocks, the reef breaks up into an array of interesting rock formations. On the other side of the reef, the rocks create impressive overhangs and huge crevices.

From about 50 yards from shore out to the seaward end of the reefs, gorgonians are plentiful—in some spots, a brilliant golden blanket of gorgonians adds bursts of color. Feather worms and colorful anemones should delight the photographer. Hunters won't be disappointed, either. Head for the outer reefs for big game fish, including halibut. Lobster (when in season), small scallops, sheepshead, and kelp bass are also available.

6

Diving in San Diego County

Diving along the coastline of San Diego County can be an exhilarating experience provided you have some experience diving the area and know specifically where to go for easy, relaxing diving. Large surf, difficult entries, and murky water are normal in the northern reaches of the coast. But don't let these factors discourage you. There are many fine reefs to dive on and plenty of sites with relatively easy access. Reefs blanketed with healthy kelp beds can be found at several locations; however, they can be as far as a quarter-mile offshore, which requires a long swim to reach the best diving. These areas include (from north to south) San Onofre, Oceanside Pier, and Carlsbad State Beach. Perhaps the best location in north San Diego County is Sea Cliff Park, also known as "Swamis." Surf here can be very large, but good visibility and kelp beds make for good diving close to shore. San Elijo State Park has an excellent beach campground, but the best diving is a long swim away through big surf. Other access points farther south can be found at Tide County Park and 13th and 8th Streets in Del Mar.

To the south of Del Mar is the northern border of the San Diego-La Jolla Underwater Park. The only marine life that can be taken from this area are abalone, clams, crab, lobster, and sea urchins. The San Diego-La Jolla Ecological Reserve is located within the boundaries of the park, and includes such popular dive sites as La Jolla Canyon, Goldfish Point, and La Jolla Cove. Enjoy your dive, but *do not* remove or disturb any marine life.

La Jolla Canyon is actually made up of two separate canyons: Scripps Canyon, recommended for experienced divers, and the La Jolla Branch, which features several vertical drops of 20–30 feet. With the excellent water visibility here, be prepared for one of the most unusual beach dives along the coast of Southern California.

The coast then turns from sandy beach to rocky cliffs along the La Jolla Bay. Access to the rocky shore can be found at Goldfish Point. Expect large crowds at nearby La Jolla Cove, one of the most popular beach locations in San Diego County. Diving here is usually good, thanks to clear waters and an abundance of marine life.

Diving along the San Diego coastline is varied. The experienced and beginner diver can find enjoyment, relaxation, and exhilaration in areas including: La Jolla Canyon (25), Goldfish Point (26), La Jolla Cove (17), Casa Pool (28), and Hospital Point (29). ➤

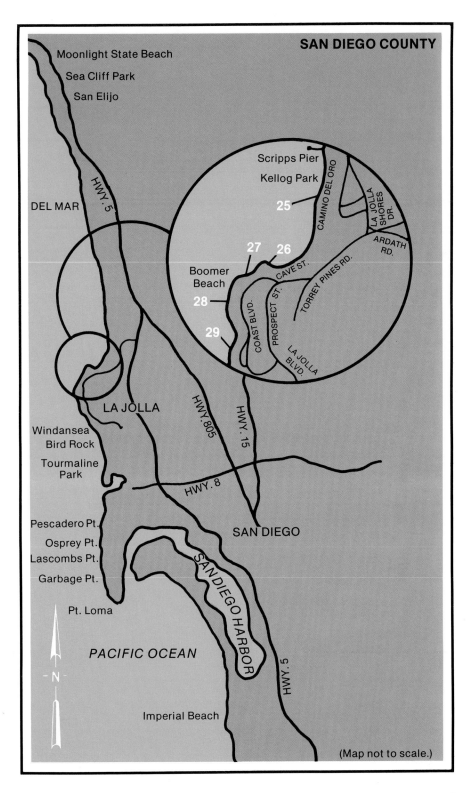

SAN DIEGO COUNTY

Moonlight State Beach

Sea Cliff Park

San Elijo

Scripps Pier

Kellog Park

25

CAMINO DEL ORO

LA JOLLA SHORES DR.

ARDATH RD.

DEL MAR

HWY. 5

27 **26**

Boomer Beach

CAVE ST.

TORREY PINES RD.

28

COAST BLVD.

PROSPECT ST.

29

LA JOLLA BLVD.

LA JOLLA

HWY. 805

HWY. 15

Windansea
Bird Rock

Tourmaline
Park

HWY. 8

SAN DIEGO

Pescadero Pt.

Osprey Pt.

Lascombs Pt.

Garbage Pt.

SAN DIEGO HARBOR

Pt. Loma

HWY. 5

- N -

PACIFIC OCEAN

Imperial Beach

(Map not to scale.)

Entry into normally clear and calm waters makes scuba diving and snorkeling at Casa Pool very popular.

From here the beach turns westward, making it susceptible to ocean conditions. There are access points at Boomer Beach and Shell Beach, but heavy surf and unpredictable rips and currents are a constant problem. Children's Pool (Casa Pool) is a small cove created by an artificial breakwater. Hospital Point is open to the weather, but under the right conditions offers very good diving in between the rock ledges. Diving at Little Point and Big Rock can be difficult due to high surf and murky water. You'll find abalone in the shallow waters at North and South Bird Rock, but not much else. Moving south, there's good beach access at Sun Gold Point and Tourmaline Park, but expect a long swim through cloudy water and high surf.

There are several points south of the Mission Bay Channel that provide beach access, but entries can be difficult and water visibility is often poor. Visibility improves slightly at Rock Slide, Rock Pile, and Garbage Points. Diving in the Point Loma kelp beds is excellent, but you can only access the site by boat. If wreck diving is your thing, head for Imperial Beach, where you'll find a sunken submarine.

Visibility in most areas of San Diego is exceptionally good. The coastline offers average visibility of 15-20 feet, but on good days it can exceed 30 feet.

Typical depth range	:	40–50 feet at edge of canyon, dropping to 200 feet
Access	:	Sandy beach
Water entry	:	Light surf
Snorkeling	:	Poor

"The training ground for the San Diego diver" is how one diver described this area after stepping from the surf at La Jolla Shores. He had just emerged from the depths of La Jolla Canyon. Twelve neophyte divers were entering the water as he and his dive buddy exited. Another pair of experienced divers bobbed in the swells offshore.

What makes La Jolla Canyon a perennial favorite of local divers at all skill levels? The answers range from good facilities to easy surf entry and excellent shore access. But let's not forget the spectacular scenery. Approximately 100 yards from shore in 35–70 feet of water, the ocean floor breaks into a steep vertical wall that extends to depths of over 800 feet.

Access to the submarine canyon is from the beach of La Jolla Shores located north of La Jolla Bay. The beach offers excellent facilities and ample parking. The best point for water entry is directly off a small lifeguard tower marked #20. The tower is located south of the main

Along the sheer walls of La Jolla Submarine Canyon are small growths of gorgonian. The gorgonian never become very large because the walls it grows on are made of clay and cannot hold the weight.

Corynactis anemones, just one of the many species living in La Jolla Canyon, is a perfect subject for the macro photographer.

lifeguard tower that's positioned at the front of the park and slightly north of Vallecitos Street. Surfers congregate north of the main tower. Stay clear of this area, as well as the area near the boat ramp, located south of Vallecitos Street at the end of Aveinda de La Playa.

As you move out from tower #20, the sandy bottom slopes moderately. Go out about 100 yards from the tower, then line yourself up so that the end of Scripp's Pier (to the north) is directly under the green building that's located on the ridge. This will place you slightly inshore from the rim of canyon in about 40 feet of water. At 50 feet there's a series of ledges that vary in height from 10–20 feet. The bottom drops off quickly to more than 300 feet. It's an exhilarating feeling to position yourself on the rim of the canyon and peer into the depths. Visibility averages 15–20 feet but can worsen with heavy surf or when plankton blooms. If there are upwellings from the canyon, visibility can improve to 30–40 feet. These upwellings also bring marine animals from the deeper waters to the rim for closer observation. Squid appear in late fall and early spring, and they in turn attract other large fish.

Several varieties of small colorful fish can be found on the clay canyon walls. Small branches of gorgonian are attached to the ledges at 65 feet, while crabs and octopusses make their homes in the holes in the clay walls. Look but don't touch! The entire area is an underwater park and ecological preserve. Marine life may not be removed or disturbed.

After you dive, feel free to freshen up at the outdoor freshwater showers located in the restroom building just behind tower #20. Then enjoy a picnic lunch in the park.

Typical depth range	:	To 30 feet
Access	:	Stairway; dirt path
Water entry	:	Surf entry from rocks
Snorkeling	:	Good

Named for the Garibaldi that congregate in the area, Goldfish Point is located at the tip of a peninsula that lies between La Jolla Cove and La Jolla Caves on the southern end of La Jolla Bay. The fish have grown accustomed to the divers and are always looking for handouts. If you're carrying food, don't be surprised if you're stalked by one of these friendly animals. Be aware that Goldfish Point is part of the La Jolla Underwater

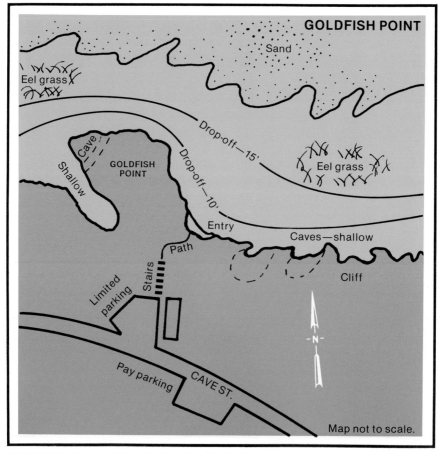

Goldfish Point is named for the abundant Garibaldi in the area. Although marine life is plentiful, divers must abide by the La Jolla Underwater Park rules, which prohibits the taking or disturbing of any marine organisms.

When calm, the water entry at Goldfish Point can be very easy. Hence, this is a popular spot for snorkelers.

Park. You're not permitted to remove or disturb any marine life. However, feel free to observe lobster, octopus, and other shy creatures!

For the photographer, starfish and anemones provide a colorful background, and the variable bottom presents some splendid photo opportunities. Reefs covered with eel grass drop to a sandy bottom 50 yards out. There are also ledges and sand channels for you to explore.

There are two ways to access the diving area adjacent to the point. The most direct route is via a path located behind the La Jolla Cave Curio Shop. A stairway and short, steep path lead to a small rock shelf at the water's edge. This is a good spot for entries, but only during very calm weather. You can also enter at La Jolla Cove and swim 200 yards to the point. There's an underground parking lot located across from the Curio Shop. Parking fees aren't cheap, but it beats driving around for hours looking for a parking spot.

Typical depth range	: To 30 feet
Access	: Stairway
Water entry	: Sandy beach
Snorkeling	: Good

La Jolla Cove is another popular spot, favored by divers and beach goers. Consequently, if you want to dive this area on summer weekends, be prepared to deal with the crowds. The cove lies on the northernmost extension of the La Jolla Peninsula. Because the cove faces north, it's well protected from the southerly swells that affect the area during the summer.

There's a series of rock ledges, reefs, and sand channels directly out from the small sandy cove. Around the point to the northwest, in an area known as "Alligator Head," marine life is abundant. Garibaldi are everywhere and, if you're lucky, you may spot a broomtail grouper. Seals are also frequent visitors, and they've grown accustomed to the divers. Moray

La Jolla Cove is a popular spot for divers. Facing north, the cove is protected from heavy swells.

Rocky reefs are a habitat for a number of colorful fish like this Garibaldi. Good access for shore diving, however, is somewhat limited.

eels, lobster, and rockfish can be found on the bottom and in the reefs. Keep in mind that La Jolla Cove lies within the San Diego-La Jolla Underwater Ecological Reserve. *Do not* remove or disturb the marine life.

On the other side of the cove, a series of rock ledges stretch close to the shore all the way to Goldfish Point. The water depth here is 30 feet. Farther out in deeper water, the bottom turns to sand where you'll find angel sharks and halibut.

Because of the crowds, it may be difficult to find a parking spot. Your best bet is to dive early in the morning or on a weekday. Parking adjacent to the Ellen Browning Scripps Memorial Park, which overlooks the cove, is limited. There are no parking meters but there is a three-hour time limit. The park offers all the amenities you'll need for post-diving activities: Restrooms, showers, telephones, picnic areas, and large grassy areas for suiting up. Water and surf conditions are posted daily at the lifeguard stand. It's advisable to check the diving conditions before you arrive. Although the cove is protected, large surf and surge are not uncommon.

The best spot to enter the water is from the small sandy beach in the middle of the cove. There are two entry points to avoid: "The hole," an indentation in the cliffs on the east side of the cove that generates rips and unpredictable currents, and a dangerous shallow reef farther to the east.

Typical depth range	: 10–30 feet
Access	: Ramps, stairway
Water entry	: Sandy beach
Snorkeling	: Good

Casa Pool is located less than a half mile south of La Jolla Cove along Coast Boulevard. This manmade cove, also known as Children's Pool, was carved out at a spot that's protected from the swells by a small sea wall, creating a pool of ocean water for children to play in. This is an excellent spot for divers to enter to reach the nearby reefs.

Depths on the reefs range from 10–30 feet. Extreme undercutting has created huge rock ledges which are inhabited by a variety of marine life. Eel grass is abundant in the shallow portions. Anemones, sponges, starfish, nudibranchs, and a variety of mollusks can be found on the ledges and rocks. Expect to find Garibaldi, senoritas, opaleye, and other fish on the reefs. You may also spot a grouper, and seals are frequent visitors. Lobster

Garibaldi, popular along most of the Southern California coastline, are friendly and fairly common. Other marine life at Casa Pool includes senoritas and groupers.

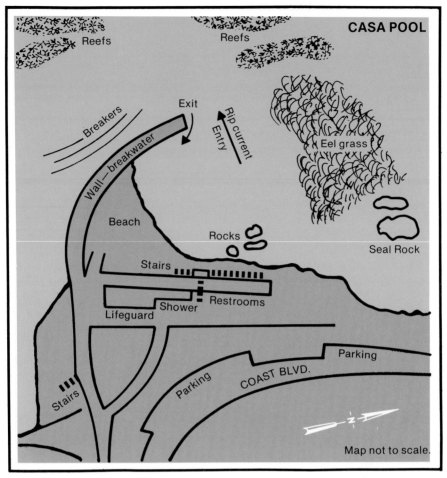

A small, calm bay near La Jolla Cove, Casa Cove is a good area for beginner divers or snorkelers. On land, facilities are well-equipped.

and abalone can sometimes be found on the outer reefs, in addition to sheepshead, calico bass, halibut, and white sea bass.

Enter Casa Pool from the small sandy beach. The strong rip running out from the end of the wall will get you to the reefs rather quickly. Returning to the cove is best done by swimming very close to the tip of the wall, where the surge will push you back into the cove. Water conditions are posted daily at the lifeguard tower.

Parking along Coast Boulevard is limited and restricted to three hours. To avoid the crowds, schedule your dive for the early morning or on a weekday. Restrooms, showers, and a drinking fountain are located below the lifeguard tower; telephones can be found behind the tower.

Typical depth range	: 10–35 feet
Access	: Stairway
Water entry	: Sandy beach
Snorkeling	: Fair

Hospital Point, sometimes called Whale View Point, is a large rocky area located less than one-half mile south of Casa Pool. There are a number of possible entry points along the rocky shore, but the one most widely used by local divers is across from 417 Coast Boulevard. A short stairway leads to a small sandy beach from where you'll enter. Especially when the surf is up, water entry can be difficult when the shallow reefs are exposed at low tide. Channels also create rips. Diving is best done at high tide.

The bottom is very shallow until about 40 yards out, where a ledge marks the drop into deeper water. The bottom gradually slopes down to 40 feet approximately 300 yards from shore. A collection of reefs interspersed with sand channels, most of which run parallel to shore, rise 10 feet above the bottom. One features a small arch you can swim through.

Even with moderate surf, surge can be a problem. You can avoid some effects of the surge by staying low in the channels between the reefs. Under good conditions, visibility averages 15–30 feet. Morays, bottom fish, octopus, lobster, and abalone can be found on the bottom offshore of the point.

Except on crowded days, parking isn't usually a problem. There are no facilities, but you'll find a few picnic tables and barbeque pits nearby.

This intimidating, yet friendly moray lives in the reef at Hospital Point. The best diving at the point is during high tide.

The rocky bottom of Hospital Point, or Whale View Point, yields to a soft, sandy beach. Water is generally calm.

7

Safety

Diving the Southern California coastline should be a very safe and enjoyable experience. Although conditions here are certainly more harsh than at some tropical islands, there is no reason why diving cannot be as safe or safer if certain factors are considered.

Cold Water. With water temperatures averaging in the 60's, hypothermia (a lowering of the body temperature due to external cold) can be a problem. Always dive with a good fitting wetsuit or drysuit, and a hood. Hypothermia can be dangerous because it accelerates respiration, deteriorates muscular coordination, and can even cloud thinking. A chilled body is also at higher risk for decompression sickness. Always allow for an extra margin of error in the dive tables when severely chilled.

Depths *should not* be a problem when diving Southern California. With only a few exceptions, depths of over 50 feet are not reachable from shore. The exceptions are the Submarine Canyons at Port Hueneme (La Jennelle Park), Redondo Beach (old Redondo Pier #2), and the La Jolla Canyon. Try to keep most of your diving depths 80 feet or shallower as this is where there is the most to see anyway. Always watch your times, depths, and tank pressure carefully on all dives, including shallow ones. Because most of your dives will be in relatively shallow water it is possible to make several dives a day. It is important to keep careful watch of your repetitive dive tables. Know how to use them and always calculate them *before* your next dive.

Entry and exit through the surf can be a hazard if not dealt with properly. See the section "Beach Diving Tips" for more information on how to deal with surf.

Hazardous Marine Animals. If you are diving California waters for the first time, several life forms may be new and strange to you. Some are dangerous while others are not, but can be so if not dealt with properly.

You are probably somewhat familiar with *sea urchins* which are very common in California. They are not poisonous but if you put your hand or knee down in the wrong place you will get stuck, even through a wetsuit or thick gloves.

The *moray eel* is another creature you may already be familiar with. The morays in California are not aggressive; however, should you shove your hand into a hole before looking you may stick it right into a moray's mouth, and they do have sharp teeth.

The *scorpionfish* (sometimes incorrectly called "sculpin") is a hazard that the non-California diver may not be familiar with. This fish is much like the stonefish, with a stinging dorsal fin spine, but the injury the scorpionfish delivers is generally more painful than harmful.

The *torpedo ray* is another unusual and dangerous California sea creature to steer clear of. These creatures are rounded in shape and have a tail with rounded fins. They are also called "Pacific electric rays" and rightfully so. They can be aggressive and will deliver an electric jolt if provoked. Other rays somewhat more common to the California coastal waters are the *thorn back ray* and the *round sting ray*. These rays have a habit of relaxing in the sand at or near the surf zone. Use caution when entering or exiting the surf because, should you step on one of these rays, its barbed stinger can cause much pain. The best method of avoiding being stung is to shuffle your fins across the sand and use caution whenever settling down on a sand bottom.

California waters have *sharks*, as do any ocean waters. The most common is the beautifully graceful blue shark. Those that have been lucky enough to encounter it have had a chance for some great photos. Although sharks are common in the open Pacific off California, shark sightings by divers near the coastline are very rare. Should you encounter a shark, treat it with the respect it deserves.

Seals pose a greater threat to Southern California divers than sharks do. Seals are playful and love to tease and dart about divers. Do not, however, attempt to touch them. Although most are quite friendly, some may take your innocent touch as an act of aggression and respond with a deep bite.

Diving Accidents. Should a diving accident occur, it is important to first stabilize the victim and then get him or her to the proper facilities as soon as possible.

If you are on shore, call 911. This is the emergency phone number now in effect throughout California. Emergency personnel will be dispatched quickly. You may also call (213) 590–2225, which is the U.S. Coast Guard Emergency Coordination Center.

If you are on a boat, call for assistance from the U.S. Coast Guard on channel 16 on a VHF marine band radio. Should they determine that the accident is serious, they will medi-vac the victim to the proper facilities. The decompression chambers presently used by the Coast Guard are located at Los Robles Hospital in Thousand Oaks, the chamber facility at the Isthmus on Catalina Island operated by USC Medical Center, and the chamber in San Diego operated by UCSD. Remember, always be sure to tell them if the accident is diving-related so that they can have the proper facilities ready.

Safety Recommendations. To make your dives along the Southern California coastline as safe and as enjoyable as possible, four things are recommended. First, consult a divemaster familiar with the waters you wish to dive. Almost all of the local dive shops have a divemaster or an instructor that is very knowledgeable. He or she can inform you as to specifics on bottom topography, marine life, and other details important to your dive.

Second, plan your dive and dive your plan. Discuss with your buddy cut-off depth (the deepest you wish to go), bottom times, direction of travel, and purpose of dive (sightseeing, hunting, photos, etc.).

Third, be in good physical condition. There is no need to be ready for a marathon, but you should be able to run around the block a couple of times with no problem. Much of the diving here is easy while some dive spots are challenging. Be sure that you are in good enough physical condition to handle the type of diving desired and any emergency that may arise.

And finally, KNOW YOUR LIMITATIONS. Diving into something that you cannot physically or mentally handle will not only make the dive unenjoyable, but it could be very dangerous. Know when to sit out the dive or to move to an easier location.

Appendix

Dive Operations

LOS ANGELES COUNTY: SOUTH BAY AND MALIBU

Scuba Haus
2501 Wilshire Blvd.
Santa Monica, CA
(213) 828-2916

Malibu Divers Inc.
21231 Pacific Coast Hwy.
Malibu, CA
(213) 456-2396

The Dive Shop
8642 Wilshire Blvd.
Beverly Hills, CA
(213) 652-4990

New England Divers
11830 W. Pico Blvd.
West Los Angeles, CA
(213) 477-5021

Marina Del Rey Divers
2539 Lincoln Blvd.
Marine Del Rey, CA
(213) 827-1131

Dive 'N Surf
504 W. Broadway
Redondo Beach, CA
(213) 372-8423

Sea D' Sea
1911 Catalina Ave.
Redondo Beach, CA
(213) 373-6355

American Institute of Diving
1901 Pacific Coast Hwy.
Lomita, CA
(213) 326-6663

LOS ANGELES COUNTY: SAN FERNANDO VALLEY

Scuba Duba Dive
7126 Reseda Blvd.
Reseda, CA
(818) 881-4545

West Coast Divers Supply
16931 Sherman Way
Van Nuys, CA
(818) 708-8136/8137

Aloha Diving Schools
7626 Tampa Ave.
Reseda, CA
(818) 343-6343

Aloha Diving Schools
2910 W. Magnolia
Burbank, CA
(818) 846-1320

Laguna Sea Sports
6959 Van Nuys Blvd.
Van Nuys, CA
(818) 787-7066

Sport Chalet Divers
920 Foothill Blvd.
La Canada, CA
(818) 790-2717

Cal Aquatics
22725 Ventura Blvd.
Woodland Hills, CA
(818) 346-4799

LOS ANGELES COUNTY: SOUTHEAST AREA

Divers Corner
11200 Old River School Rd.
Downey, CA
(213) 927-1417

New England Divers
4148 Viking Way
Long Beach, CA
(213) 421-8939, (714) 827-5110

Scuba Schools of Long Beach
4740 Pacific Coast Hwy.
Long Beach, CA
(213) 494-4740

LOS ANGELES COUNTY: NORTHEAST AREA

Sport Diving West, Inc.
11501 Whittier Blvd.
Whittier, CA
(213) 692-7373

Divers West
2695 Foothill Blvd.
#A, Pasadena, CA
(818) 796-4287

Gucciones Scuba Habitat
3220-B S. Brea Canyon Rd.
Diamond Bar, CA
(714) 594-7927

Southern California Diving Center
1121 S. Glendora Ave.
W. Covina, CA
(818) 338-8863

SAN BERNARDINO COUNTY

Sea-To-Sea Scuba School
10950 S. Mt. Vernon Ave.
Colton, CA
(714) 825-2502

Undersea Showcase
1335 W. Foothill Blvd.
Upland, CA
(714) 946-2266

RIVERSIDE COUNTY

Laguna Sea Sports
6343 Magnolia Blvd.
Riverside, CA
(714) 683-6244

SANTA BARBARA COUNTY

The Dive Shop of Santa Maria
1975 B. South Broadway
Santa Maria, CA
(805) 922-0076

Dive West Sports
115 W. Main
Santa Maria, CA
(805) 925-5878

Watersports Unltd.
732 North H St.
Lompoc, CA
(805) 736-1800

Bob's Diving Locker
500 Botello Road
Goleta, CA
(805) 967-4456

Divers Supply of Santa Barbara
5854 Hollister Ave.
Goleta, CA
(805) 964-0180

Aquatics of Santa Barbara
5370 Hollister #3
Santa Barbara, CA
(805) 964-8689

Divers Den
22 Anacapa St.
Santa Barbara, CA
(805) 963-8917

Underwater Sports
Breakwater Harbor
Santa Barbara, CA
(805) 962-5400

VENTURA COUNTY

Far West Marine Center
Thousand Oaks
Simi Valley, Canyon Country, CA

(805) 495-3600, (805) 522-2628,
(805) 252-6955

Aquatics
295 Channel Islands Blvd.
Port Hueneme, CA
(805) 984-DIVE

Ocean Antics
2359 E. Thompson
Ventura, CA
(805) 652-1600

Ventura Scuba School
1559 Spinnaker #108
Ventura, CA
(805) 656-0167

Aqua Ventures
1001 S. Harbor Blvd.
Oxnard, CA
(805) 985-8861

Poncho's Dive & Tackle
3600 Cabazone Way
Oxnard, CA
(805) 985-4788

Aqua Ventures
2172 Pickwick Dr.
Camarillo, CA
(805) 647-8344

Scuba Luv
704 Thousand Oaks Blvd.
Thousand Oaks, CA
(805) 496-1014

ORANGE COUNTY: NORTHERN AREA

Openwater Habitat Marine School
411 South Main St.
Orange, CA
1-800-334,6467, (714) 633-7283

Diver's Mart
2036 W. Whittier
La Habra, CA
(213) 694-1311

Scuba Toys
9547 Valley View
Cypress, CA
(714) 527-0430

Scuba Toys, Too
1640 W. Lincoln
Anaheim, CA
(714) 956-5540

Sea Ventures
350 E. Orangethorpe #2
Placentia, CA
(714) 993-3211

Scuba World
1706 Tustin
Orange, CA
(714) 998-6382

Ocean Sports Ltd.
3141 Yorba Linda Blvd.
Fullerton, CA
(714) 996-1970

ORANGE COUNTY: SOUTHERN AREA

Black Barts Aquatics
34145 Coast Hwy.
Dana Point, CA
(714) 496-5891

Black Barts Aquatics
24882 Muirlands
El Toro, CA
(714) 855-2323

Aquatic Center
4535 Coast Hwy.
Newport Beach, CA
(714) 650-5440

Adventures in Diving
31678 Coast Hwy.
South Laguna, CA
(714) 499-4517

Mr. Scuba
1031 S. Coast Hwy.
Laguna Beach, CA
(714) 494-4146

The Dive Shop
16475 Harbor Blvd.
Fountain Valley, CA
(714) 531-5838

National Scuba
16442 A Gothard St.
Huntington Beach, CA
(714) 847-4386

Sport Chalet Divers
16242 Beach Blvd.
Huntington Beach, CA
(714) 848-0988

Laguna Sea Sports
2146 Newport Blvd.
Costa Mesa, CA
(714) 645-5820

Laguna Sea Sports
925 N. Coast Hwy.
Laguna Beach, CA
(714) 494-6965

Ocean Rhythm
27601 Forbes Rd. #19
Laguna Miguel, CA
(714) 582-3882

Ocean Sports Ltd.
5046 Edinger Ave.
Huntington Beach, CA
(213) 592-2506, (714) 840-4840

SAN DIEGO COUNTY: NORTHERN AREA

Diving Locker Aquatics
348 East Grand
Escondido, CA
(619) 746-8980

Ocean Enterprises
267 El Camino Real
Encinitas, CA
(619) 942-3661

Diving Locker Aquatics
405 N. Highway 101
Solana Beach, CA
(619) 755-6822

Sport Chalet Divers
Vineyard Shopping Center
Escondido, CA
(619) 746-5958

SAN DIEGO COUNTY: SOUTHERN AREA

Water Education Training (W.E.T.)
7094 Miramar Rd.
San Diego, CA
(619) 578-DIVE (3483)

San Diego Divers Supply
7522 La Jolla Blvd.
La Jolla, CA
(619) 459-2691

Diving Locker Aquatics
1020 Grand Ave.
San Diego, CA
(619) 272-1120

New England Divers
3860 Rosecrans St.
San Diego, CA
(619) 298-0531

Ocean Enterprises
4646 Convoy St.
San Diego, CA
(619) 565-6054

San Diego Divers Supply
4004 Sports Arena Blvd.
San Diego, CA
(619) 224-3439

National City Divers Supply
105 W. 18th
National City, CA
(619) 477-5946

Ocean Stuff Dive Shop
2434 South Port Way #E
National City, CA
(619) 477-5946

Ward's Dry Dock
2198 Hwy. 86
El Centro, CA
(619) 352-2033

Sports Chalet Divers
5500 Grossmont Ctr. Dr.
La Mesa, CA
(619) 463-9381

Surf and Dive Reports

Santa Barbara County
(805) 962-SURF

Ventura County
(805) 644-8338

Los Angeles County
North: (213) 457-9701
South: (213) 379-8471

Orange County
(714) 650-5783

San Diego County
(619) 225-9492

California Department of Fish and Game
(for current fish and game regulations)
1416 9th St.
Sacramento, CA 95814
(213) 590-5132

Further Reading:

Gotshall, D. *Pacific Coast Inshore Fishes.* Los Osos, California: Sea Challengers; Ventura, California: Western Marine Enterprises

California Diving News monthly publication dedicated to California sport diving, P.O. Box 11231, Torrance, CA 90510

Index